Carry Me Home

Carry Me Home

A personal story about tragedy, transformation and the search for true wholeness

CATHERINE LUCAS

MICHAEL JOSEPH
an imprint of
PENGUIN BOOKS

MICHAEL JOSEPH

Published by the Penguin Group
Penguin Books Ltd, 80 Strand, London WC2R ORL, England
Penguin Group (USA) Inc., 375 Hudson Street, New York, New York 10014, USA
Penguin Group (Canada), 10 Alcorn Avenue, Toronto, Ontario, Canada M4V 3B2
(a division of Pearson Penguin Canada Inc.)
Penguin Ireland, 25 St Stephen's Green, Dublin 2, Ireland (a division of Penguin Books Ltd)
Penguin Group (Australia), 250 Camberwell Road, Camberwell, Victoria 3124, Australia
(a division of Pearson Australia Group Pty Ltd)
Penguin Books India Pvt Ltd, 11 Community Centre,
Panchsheel Park, New Delhi – 110 017, India
Penguin Group (NZ), cnr Airborne and Rosedale Roads, Albany,
Auckland 1310, New Zealand (a division of Pearson New Zealand Ltd)
Penguin Books (South Africa) (Pty) Ltd, 24 Sturdee Avenue,
Rosebank 2196, South Africa

Penguin Books Ltd, Registered Offices: 80 Strand, London WC2R ORL, England

www.penguin.com

First published 2005
2

Set in 12/14.75pt Bembo
Typeset by Palimpsest Book Production Limited, Polmont, Stirlingshire
Printed in Great Britain by Clays Ltd, St Ives plc

A CIP catalogue record for this book is available from the British Library

ISBN 0-718-14803-7

To Tate.

And to all of you who are confused or hurt or lost: no matter where you are or what has happened it *is* possible to heal – may you be happy, may you be at peace, may you live with love, may you discover the source of your being – the one light within us all.

Acknowledgements

My deepest love and appreciation go to Cyril, Bonnie, Geoff, Vicki, Valentine, La and Oliver – thank you for being my family; to my godmother, Joan, for initiating me into boundless joy and beauty; to Steve, Susie, William and Jonathon for seeing the real me; to my friends in England and California for their unfailing love and encouragement; to all my teachers, who have shown up in many different disguises, especially the three 'M's – Mark, Matt and Mike; to Caroline Knight, without whose faith, friendship and editorial insight this book would not have been written. And my heartfelt thanks go to my agents Toby Eady and Jessica Woollard for their support and excellent advice, and to Kate Adams and her team at Michael Joseph for their vision and dedication.

Preface

'Do you think Catherine realizes?'

Two women stood together in the courtyard of the house I grew up in. Beyond them steps led down to the lawn, bathed in afternoon sunlight, where other groups of people gathered, holding cups of tea, little fingers cocked in the proper English manner, as they sipped and chatted.

'I don't know,' the second woman replied. 'Perhaps she is still in shock.'

I was passing through the doorway behind them, a plate of sandwiches in my hand and I stopped still in amazement.

'Do I realize?' I wanted to scream. 'Do any of you realize? Do any of you have the faintest idea what a nightmare this is?'

For this was no ordinary tea party. It was my mother's funeral. She had died a few days before in a blinding crash of glass and smashing steel, right next to me. Her body slumped on mine, her blood dripping into my eyes, thicker than tears. She was giving me a driving lesson when we had the accident. She was fifty-six years old and I was seventeen. In a matter of moments my world shattered. My mother was dead and I was left to deal with the wreckage and I had absolutely no idea how to do that.

For years after the accident I pushed the pain away because I didn't know how else to deal with it.

Unfortunately by doing so I just prolonged it, for it didn't magically go away. Instead it turned into a living wound, festering beneath my skin. Although I did not, could not admit it, even to myself, my life was a misery because of the unexpressed grief and guilt I carried. I was trapped – imprisoned by a past I did not know how to release or heal.

And not just my mother's death, but the whole of my past – the fears and hurts of childhood, the rules and conditioning of my family and culture – had all solidified in my mind, as strong and rigid as the bars of any prison. Surely, I thought to myself one day in my early twenties, life does not have to be like this? I have since discovered that it doesn't.

The greatest gift in the pain of my early years and perhaps especially that of my mother's death was that I was hurting so badly it forced me to embark on a healing journey. Like all human beings, I wanted to be happy and I was determined to find out how I could be. Over time this search revealed itself to be a spiritual journey driven by a much deeper longing, a hunger in my soul for love and truth and wholeness.

This longing was the pull towards the great mystery we often refer to as God. I don't mean the God of the Bible, I mean the invisible and ineffable realm of spirit which is the source of all life. So although the pain was an incentive to begin the process of healing, it was not my true reason for making this journey. For I don't believe the desire to grow and fulfil our true potential comes from being wounded; I believe it is programmed into the very fabric of being human. An acorn is destined to grow into an oak tree, a lion cub into a lion. It is our destiny as human beings to wake up, to become whole, to embody our true spirit.

So mine is a story about the journey to wholeness. It is about learning to heal emotionally and to turn the lead of tragedy into the gold of transformation. It is about becoming authentic and real, breaking free from the cage of my ego and conditioning. It is about learning to live consciously by freeing myself from the chains of habit and the past. It is about choosing to live a life of love, moment to moment. It is about letting the deepest longing of my soul carry me home. Above all it is about awakening spiritually and learning to celebrate and rejoice in the light and spirit that is in all things.

1. The Accident

I sat on the grass bank outside my high school, waiting for my mother, or Tate as we all called her, to come and pick me up. The sun soaked through my uniform, warming my skin, and I pulled off my school tie and unbuttoned the collar of my white shirt as I chatted and laughed with my friends. It was one of those gorgeous, effortless days. It was 1982 and the summer term was nearly over. I was seventeen and feeling that first surge of power and the sense of being on the cusp of something momentous that comes with growing up and becoming independent.

I was also excited that Tate was coming to collect me. It was so much nicer than catching the bus, and I was learning to drive, so this was another chance to practise. I thought of all the things I would do when I got home – feed and water the horses, maybe go for a ride . . . I was especially looking forward to spending the evening with Tate. My father and brother were away in America for a couple of weeks on business and it was wonderful to spend time with her alone. Lately our relationship had shifted and deepened: we were no longer talking to each other as mother and child, but as two women confiding in each other, and I felt as if I was just getting to know her.

She pulled up in our old blue minivan, with two of our dogs in the back: Hercules, a yellow Labrador and Mickey Mouse, a Jack Russell terrier. Tate climbed over to the passenger seat while I jumped in the driver's side. We didn't stop to kiss or hug each other, because we simply never did that, but by her brilliant smile I knew immediately she was in a good mood. We set off, winding our way through the back streets of the little town where I went to school, to the main road that led home. It was long and straight for miles and I had driven it many times. My sweater was draped over my shoulders and I started to get too hot. I thought that it would be easy to pull it off, so I reached up with my right hand. It didn't come easily and I tugged at it.

Suddenly my mother screamed and grabbed hold of the wheel. Without noticing I had swerved towards the hedge on the left and she tried to straighten the car. But she over-steered and we veered violently to the right, crossing over the centre line. I was so frightened I let go of the wheel, relieved that she had taken control, and she tried again to straighten the car, steering sharply to the left. As we crossed the grass verge and went into the ditch I distinctly remember thinking, Thank God for that, we are going to be all right.

It seemed so innocent and simple. A twist this way, a turn that, and we were driving so slowly, no more than thirty miles an hour, that I really felt a huge sense of relief. Still, there was a horrendous noise as we crashed nose first into the ditch. Glass exploded all around me and I heard the dogs leap out of one of the windows. Somehow I ended up crouched on the floor. I was covered in petrol. The engine was still running and I was terrified – more terrified than I could ever have imagined feeling – that the car was going to burst into flames at any moment.

There was a heavy weight pressing down on top of me.

I tried to see what it was, but my eyes were stinging and burning and I couldn't open them. 'Mummy! Mummy!' I called out. But she didn't answer. The silence was devastating. I knew immediately that she was dead. If she had been alive she would have been screaming and her silence was more awful than her screams could ever have been. I realized she must be lying on top of me, pinning me to the floor, and I crouched there for what felt like eternity, feeling the soft, heavy dripping of blood from her body on to mine.

Still the engine raced, high-pitched and out of control. I fumbled around with one hand, trying to find the key, but it was hopeless. I wasn't even really sure where I was in the car, let alone where to find the ignition, so I just waited, silently. My mind went into free fall. I was completely conscious and I knew what had happened, but I simply couldn't take it in. The facts floated around my mind – I had killed my mother, I was in danger of burning to death, I couldn't see, I couldn't move – but they were like leaves swirling in water and I couldn't make sense of anything.

I have no idea how long I was there before I heard voices outside the car. They were warm and reassuring: 'Don't worry, you'll be fine. We'll get you out in just a moment . . .'

The words 'you'll be fine' dropped into my mind's swirl, as meaningless as everything else. How could I possibly be fine? I had just killed my mother. She was lying on top of me, the taste of her blood in my mouth. What kind of nightmare world had I entered where this was fine?

I felt hands on me, lifting me out of the car. I stumbled

out, rubbing my eyes: the sunshine was blinding and the world was shockingly normal. The fields rolled away to either side, the sky was still blue, the road was firm under my feet. There were two ambulances on the other side of the road and a paramedic led me towards one of them. Once inside he began to ask me questions. What was my name? Who was in the car with me? Who should they contact?

In my imagination I could hear the phones ringing as I gave him names and contact numbers for my sister and aunt. I could hear their welcoming and curious, 'Hello!' Hear the slight pause, as a strange voice on the end of the line prepared itself to say, 'I'm sorry, there has been an accident . . .' I could see them standing there, slowly putting down the receiver, their world shattered, and I could feel their shock and grief far more deeply than I could feel my own. I didn't know the contact number for my father and brother in America, but I remembered that it was written on a piece of paper in the kitchen. Who would call them?

The questions seemed endless and I had a question too: 'Is she dead?' 'Is she dead?' 'Is she dead?'

Each time the paramedic answered, 'I don't know.'

'I know!' I wanted to scream. 'I know!' But the truth was still too much to bear, so I didn't say anything and we sat there, he and I, looking out of the open door on to the road. Finally two men appeared. They were carrying a long, white, heavy zip-up plastic bag, which they laid down on the grass beside the other ambulance. I looked at it, knowing and not wanting to know.

'Is she dead?' I asked.

'I don't know,' came the reply.

'Well if she's not dead,' I said, 'why have they put her in that plastic bag?'

It was the last time I saw my mother – lying in a plastic bag on the side of the road. Moments later, the door to my ambulance closed and we drove away. At the hospital I was taken into casualty. Someone must have undressed me, for the next thing I remember is lying on a table in a hospital gown, looking up at a nurse. She was picking fragments of glass out of my face, but the cuts were only minor and they were the only physical injuries I had.

A doctor came up to the table and stood a few feet away. He didn't take my hand or tell me his name, he just said, 'I have some bad news for you. Your mother is dead.' Even though his words only confirmed what I already knew, they made it real in some way and it was as if a glass wall that had separated me from what was happening lifted away and I was plunged deeper into the nightmare. I was too shocked and numb to feel anything, let alone cry, but the nurse did, and I remember looking up at the tears running down her face and thinking, It must be bad, even the nurse is crying.

I was put in a private room and I lay in bed, shocked and silent. Inwardly I wanted to start screaming and never stop; outwardly I was paralysed and numb with guilt. I kept repeating these words to myself: I have killed my mother. It was incomprehensible, impossible to take in; impossible to believe what had actually happened. Yet it had happened, and over and over again I woke from the momentary soothing trance of disbelief into the same unbearable knowledge. The last moments in the car with her replayed again and again in my mind's eye, torturing me with what might have been, yet each time telling the same unalterable story: my mother was dead and I had killed her.

I wished that I was dead too. Although not too, instead of. God! I just wished that I was dead.

But I wasn't and so, somehow, I had to get through it. All I knew was that I didn't deserve any sympathy, I didn't deserve to grieve, I didn't deserve to cry, I didn't deserve to be helped or comforted, I didn't deserve anything because I had killed her. Instead, I felt I had to make amends as best I could for the terrible thing I had done. I had taken my mother's life from her; stolen this woman who was wife, mother, sister, friend to so many. How could I ever make up for that?

'Oh darling,' my aunt La said when she arrived, 'what a terrible thing to happen, are you all right?'

'I'm fine,' I said, sitting up and forcing myself to appear OK. 'Really, I am fine. I am just so sorry, so sorry, so sorry.'

Then Bonnie, my sister, raced in. 'Thank God you aren't hurt!' she began. 'It wasn't your fault – no matter what happened, it wasn't your fault. You know how accident-prone Tate was, something like this was bound to happen one day – I'm just so sorry you were involved.' Her words drifted past me, petals blowing on a breeze, giving me no comfort, because inside I knew the truth and she didn't.

'But it is my fault,' I replied, my throat so tight I could barely breathe, let alone squeeze words out of it. 'I made a mistake that caused the accident, so it is my fault.'

More people came and went. I have little memory of what was said or what happened. I was so numb everything just washed over me and the effort of holding myself together and pretending to be OK took all the energy I had. I do remember one of my teachers coming and saying to me, 'Don't let this put you off driving, Catherine, your mother wanted you to learn to drive. It is really important you don't give up.' And I remember a male nurse who sat with me during the first evening after all my visitors had been and gone. He just sat quietly on a chair at the end of the bed, not saying or doing anything, simply being with me. I felt so comforted by his presence that I finally slept.

The person I most dreaded seeing was my father. I knew it would take at least a day for him and Geoff to get back from America and I imagined how awful their journey would be. I kept thinking about what to say to him. What was there I could say? No one in my family ever talked about emotions, so I couldn't possibly tell him how desperate I was feeling. In fact, growing up in a turbulent and tempestuous family environment I had learnt never to say how I felt in order to avoid causing more trouble. Instead I just tried to be good and to please everyone according to their individual requirements, like a chameleon changing colour to suit its environment. All my life I had tried to live up to my father's expectations, to be good enough and intelligent enough to deserve his love. Now I had done something so unforgivably stupid that I was sure there could be no chance of him ever loving me again. And it wasn't just that I had done something stupid, like crash the car – I had killed his wife. His wife!

We finally met in the hospital hallway. I remember us walking towards each other. Tears were pouring down my face and I felt as if my heart was breaking. I remember him holding me and asking me if I was all right, but I don't remember what else he said or how I replied. All my effort and concentration went into holding myself together, so that I didn't break down completely. But inside I was dying, literally dying – and I desperately hoped that he would see. Hoped he would step from behind the wall of his own pain and reach out and comfort me. But he couldn't. And neither could I. If I had broken down, there in the hospital hallway, it is just possible that my father would have broken down too, and I knew that wouldn't do at all.

After a couple of days in hospital I went home. It was a glorious, sunny July day, the dogs were outside, happy and welcoming, the roses in the courtyard were blooming, the kitchen was just the same, but my mother was not there. However there were plenty of other people who had arrived to help and the house was full of bustle and activity, from making lunch to planning the funeral. These were people I had known all my life, but I was too ashamed to even look at them and their smiling busyness only added to my sense of separation. No one showed any grief and I followed their example. Clearly if they were all making the best of it, there was no excuse for me, who had caused it all, to break down or demand attention.

A family friend took me shopping for something to wear to the funeral and with the best of intentions tried to make it fun. 'Let's find something glamorous,' she said. I wanted to wear the skirt I had been wearing on the day of the accident. It was dark blue, so suitable for the occasion. It was also ripped and bloodstained, and maybe I hoped it would prompt someone to ask me what had actually happened. But I played along and we bought a rather sophisticated knee-length navy dress, which everyone said I looked wonderful in. As if it fucking matters, I thought bitterly, as I watched myself become more and more hopelessly lost in the surreal gap between how I behaved on the outside and how I felt on the inside.

Of course people asked me how the accident happened, but no one asked me what it was like or how it felt. No one said, 'It must have been terrifying, would you like to tell me about it?' Or, 'If I was in your shoes, I would be feeling so guilty – are you?' Perhaps they simply didn't know what to say or how to say it. Perhaps they thought it would remind me or make it worse. Or perhaps people did ask me and I couldn't bear to tell them, because I believed it was too terrible to tell, too horrific to burden anyone else with ever.

So I simply went through the motions, moving robot-like through the tasks of each day, with as much seeming normality as I could muster. I ate cornflakes for breakfast, made sandwiches for lunch, smiled and chatted with people who came to visit. At times I did wonder, Is this how it is meant to be when your mother dies? Is this what it is like? Aren't you supposed to cry or something? I really didn't know. But then I would remember that it was my fault and so I didn't deserve to cry anyway.

Guilt is such a powerful feeling with its own logic, rules and reality, that for years I honestly believed that I didn't have any right to grieve because of the terrible thing that I had done. But it wasn't just guilt that prevented me from crying. I was also terrified by the intensity of my emotions. Inside a storm was raging of shame, horror, disbelief and loss, and I thought that if I let myself really feel what was going on it would annihilate me. So I coped in the only way I could – by burying my feelings as deeply as possible. I was like a dog burying a bone, which I would later, many years later, have to painstakingly excavate. But at the time I didn't have any alternative. I had spent my whole childhood learning how not to express my emotions, so I didn't know that feeling is an essential part of healing. Nor did I know that there was such a thing as a grieving process or techniques for dealing with trauma. And neither did anyone else.

Although in the first few days after the accident someone did suggest that I see a psychiatrist. I was completely opposed to the idea because I felt so guilty and undeserving, and given my family's aversion to any kind of emotional disclosure, it didn't take much on my part to veto it. However my family were seriously concerned, both about me and about what to do with me, and it was decided that I needed a distraction. So I was enrolled for a six-week cordon bleu cookery course in London. It was presented to me as a fait accompli.

'It's a great opportunity,' Bonnie said, trying to convince me. 'It will come in really useful when you are older.'

My father agreed. 'Besides,' he added, the truth barely concealed by his joking tone, 'someone has got to know how to cook around here.'

Within ten days of Tate's death, I found myself in London, staying with Della, the woman who had taken me shopping for something to wear to the funeral. Early on Monday morning I dutifully arrived at the cookery school along with seventy other people. We were shown into a large demonstration kitchen, with rows of chairs arranged in front of a kitchen counter. A white folder, on top of which was placed a neatly folded blue-and-white striped apron, lay on each chair. I took a seat and settled down to watch a demonstration of how to make quiche Lorraine. At times I glanced around the room at my new companions. At others I just stared at my lap trying to make some sense of what was happening to me.

If it had been impossible for me to tell my family how I was really feeling, now, surrounded by a group of strangers, it was completely out of the question. I buried my emotions deeper still and navigated my way through each day on autopilot as if everything were perfectly normal. In fact at times the sheer anonymity was a relief, and pretending to be OK wasn't nearly as difficult as it had been at home. I forgot about the accident for hours at a time and to my surprise I found that I enjoyed learning to cook.

I even had fun being in London. I loved looking at everything, the buildings, the shops, the clothes and the self-conscious beauty of the people as they paraded down the street. Della's house was on a street just off the King's Road, and in the evening as I wove my way through the crowds of shoppers, diners and theatregoers, I couldn't help but notice how much vitality there was all around me. Life as I knew it had come to a sudden end – but not all life had ended, and realizing this gave me courage.

It didn't take long to find out how uncomfortable people were with death. In the course of conversation people constantly asked me where I was from, what my family did, why I was doing the cookery course. I would steer my way through these enquiries as dexterously as possible, but eventually we would come to the inevitable question: 'And what about your mother?'

'Oh,' I would say, struggling to keep my voice level as the image of her lying in the white plastic bag flashed before my eyes, 'she is dead.' Even as I said it, it still seemed impossible and each time I heard the words echo in my ears, I wondered, Have I gone mad or is that really true?

For many people that was enough and they would back off immediately. But there were a few intrepid souls who dared to go further. I remember sitting on the train going back home after my first week in London. Sitting opposite was an extremely good-looking young man, maybe four or five years older than me. He started chatting and I was flattered that he wanted to talk to me.

We soon came to the where-is-your-mother question. I answered and waited, expecting him to do a sharp U-turn, but he went on: 'How did she die?'

'In a car crash,' I answered very simply and with a small surge of hope, thinking maybe it was OK to talk about this after all.

'How long ago did she die?'

I glanced up at him nervously. This was new territory. Could it possibly be all right to venture into it? 'About two weeks ago,' I replied.

He choked. 'Two weeks? Did you say two weeks?'

I nodded.

'Oh, my God.'

The conversation dried up and his gaze, which had previously been locked on me, was now fixed firmly on the view outside the window. I felt like a leper, shunned and ashamed and so desperately alone. It is simply not safe to talk about this, I told myself, and I resolved to keep my mother's death hidden.

Then a couple of weeks later I was assigned a different cooking partner in another part of the kitchen. She and I were working away busily, but I couldn't help overhearing a man called Roger, who was working nearby. He was complaining bitterly that his mother was dying. His words caught at me like splinters of glass and by the time tears were dripping into my carefully whipped chocolate mousse I couldn't stand it any more.

'If you're so worried about it, why don't you go and be with her?' I asked.

He turned towards me, somewhat taken aback, and said, 'Oh, you couldn't possibly understand.'

'Yes,' I said, in a strangled voice, my own grief crouched like an animal waiting to spring, 'I think I can. My mother died a month ago and I know I would give anything just to spend another minute with her. Go and tell your mother all the things you have never been able to say – don't wait until it is too late.'

He looked at me incredulously for a moment, words forming and dying away in his mouth unspoken. Without replying, he put down his spoon, took off his apron, walked out of class and didn't come back.

I watched him go with a mixture of envy and satisfaction. Jealous that he at least could do what I could not – say goodbye. Yet happy that someone else might be spared the terrible feelings of remorse I now lived with because of all the things that were left unsaid. On top of the guilt I felt, I was reeling – my whole family was reeling – from the trauma caused by the fact that my mother's life had been ripped away so suddenly. I so longed to see her again. Just a minute to say, 'I love you. I'm sorry. Thank you.' That would have been enough. The shocked silence lingered after Roger left and with an effort I brought my thoughts back to the task in hand and finished whipping my mousse.

One weekend instead of going home I went to visit a friend called Claire, who I met when I went to boarding school between the ages of thirteen and sixteen. Her parents lived abroad and so she had often come to stay with me during school breaks and had decided to adopt my family. I could never figure out why she wanted to be a part of us when we seemed so crazy to me, but there it was, she did.

On the Saturday afternoon we went for a walk down a country lane near her house, through a tunnel of green summer leaves and honeysuckle, with the drowsy buzz of insects hovering in the air above us. She was quiet for a while before she finally said, 'I was really hurt that you didn't invite me to the funeral. You know how much I loved your mother and I would like to have said good-bye to her. Why didn't you want me to be there?'

'Oh Claire,' I said, 'funerals aren't by invitation – they're open to everyone. I would have loved it if you'd come. In fact I wondered why you didn't.'

'Oh,' she said, 'I didn't know. And I still don't know what happened. Can you tell me?'

I answered as if I was a reporter relating the facts. I explained about the sweater, the scream, the turning of the wheel, my relief, the crash, the silence. The rest of the details – the terror, the engine, the blood, the shatter-ing knowledge that she was dead – I kept secret.

'How do you feel?' Claire asked, when I had finished describing the accident. We walked on down the lane as

I wrestled with myself about how to answer this question. Although I had learnt to hide my feelings I didn't like deliberately lying.

'I feel terrible,' I said at last, relieved to say it. 'I would do anything for it not to have happened. But of course there is nothing I can do and I feel so guilty that honestly, most of the time, I wish I was dead too.'

'Catherine, I am sure it wasn't your fault,' Claire said, stopping me as we walked and taking hold of my arm.

'That's what everyone says,' I replied. 'It doesn't help. You weren't in the car, none of you were. If I hadn't made a mistake she wouldn't be dead: it is as simple as that.'

2. Home

The cookery course ended and I came home, back to the Isle of Wight, to the house I had lived in since I was five years old. We lived – my mother and father; my sister Bonnie, who was twelve years older than me; my brother Geoff, six years older than me, and I – in an old, rambling stone house called Dodpits House. It was surrounded by a large garden and fields, with barns and stables and animals of all kinds – dogs, cats, guinea pigs, chickens, horses. When my father bought the house it was completely derelict. The roof had fallen in, the ceilings had collapsed, the doors were hanging off their hinges and local kids had broken in to cover the walls in graffiti.

It took my parents years of hard work, inside and out – building walls, paving courtyards, planting the garden, wallpapering, painting, panelling and polishing – to turn it into a beautiful home. Architecturally, it was a curious mix: a sixteenth-century cottage with a large, formal Georgian wing attached to it, forming an L-shape. The cottage was really the heart of the house, because it contained the kitchen, with its low wooden beams, flag-stone floor, oil-fired Aga, the dogs and cats, and my mother, around whom we all gravitated like planets round the sun.

Without her there, I took over the food shopping and most of the cooking and then at the beginning of September I went back to school. My uniform, my school bag, my books all felt like the belongings of the little girl I no longer was. I felt the curious gaze of my schoolmates and once more picked my way carefully along the edge of a vast gulf of silence and questions that couldn't be asked or answered.

Life soon began to settle into a routine of school, shopping and cooking. Behind the routine was an appalling emptiness. I missed my mother so much. At the same time it was still incredible to me that she was dead. I was in the habit of remembering all the funny little things that people said or did during the day to share with her when I got home. Each time I thought, Oh, I must tell that to Tate, it was like a slap in the face when I realized she was no longer there to tell it to. Or I would see something that she liked, a tiny thing like a packet of her favourite mint humbugs, and remember with a sickening jolt that there was no point in buying it.

I was haunted by flashbacks. No matter what I was doing – writing an essay for an English class, grooming the horses or chopping vegetables – images from the accident sprang into my mind. I was unable to stop myself from reliving it over and over again, desperately looking for a way to make it different. To make it OK. To rewrite the ending and bring her back. And every time I went through it, it just confirmed the fact that it was my fault and reinforced the guilt I felt.

It wasn't the first time I had made a mistake driving – there had been several occasions when I got distracted and she had had to sharply remind me to concentrate. Once she even said, 'Watch out, or you'll kill something one day!' Now her words wrapped round me like barbed wire. I was sure she would be angry with me. Sure she would blame me. Sure she wouldn't forgive me. Much as I wanted to see her again, I actually lived in terror of her reappearing and for years I dreaded going to bed at night, because I felt sure it was only a matter of time before she came back and accused me of killing her.

One Saturday evening, a couple of months after the accident, I watched an old black-and-white horror film on television with Geoff and his friend Martin. By the end of it I was frightened and upset. 'Why do you have to be so stupid?' Geoff asked. 'It's only a film and besides there are no such things as ghosts.' This was a familiar argument. I was convinced that our house was haunted, while Dad and Geoff dismissed this feeling as a figment of my imagination.

'How do you know?' I retorted and then burst into tears and fled up to my room, sobbing.

A few minutes later Martin knocked on my bedroom door and came in. 'What's the matter?' he asked. 'Why are you so upset?' There was a note of real concern in his voice.

'You wouldn't understand,' I said.

'Try me,' he answered.

'I can't. I can't bear to tell you.'

'Whatever it is,' he said, 'it can't be that bad.'

'It is that bad,' I replied, with more tears.

Finally, reluctantly, I told him I was frightened that Tate was going to appear and accuse me of killing her.

'Oh, Bebe,' he said, using my family nickname, 'surely you don't believe that?'

'Yes I do. It's my fault she's dead, and you don't know what she was like. How angry she got. She will never forgive me. And I know she's here – I can feel her.'

'There is nothing to forgive – it wasn't your fault,' he said, and he tried to put his arm around me, but I wriggled away. I could feel scalding tears, messengers of a much deeper pain, pricking in my eyes and I couldn't bear to be comforted. Instead with a tremendous effort I regained control, thanked him for coming up and told him I was OK.

'Are you sure?' he asked, not at all convinced, and I nodded, struggling to remain composed until he had gone.

I got into bed and lay there distraught and exhausted. As usual my mind was racing, frantically trying to make sense of everything and most importantly of all trying to understand this woman, my mother, who had vanished so suddenly from my life and who I was still so afraid of.

She was about five foot five, petite and thin, with dark-brown curly hair, dark-brown extremely expressive eyes, thick menacing eyebrows and a dazzling smile. She was beautiful in an unconventional way, and she had a charm and vitality and spontaneity that were irresistible. She could make even the most mundane activities, like going shopping for groceries, seem wild and exciting. She was a full-time mother and housewife, although I doubt if she would have called herself that.

When I was a little girl, she used to lay my school uniform on the Aga to get warm on cold winter mornings. I would come down in my nightie to get dressed in the kitchen and she would help button me into the neatly ironed white shirt and grey tunic. As she tied my tie her face would be a mixture of concentration and impatience. We were usually late, because I was always reluctant to get out of my cosy, safe bed and even less keen to go to school. When I was buttoned and tied she would hand me a marmalade toast sandwich and bundle me outside to wait for the friends who gave me a lift to school. We would stand together as I took my first bite of toast, the tang of marmalade that she had made sharp in my mouth and the ooze of butter soft as it dribbled down my fingers.

She was a great cook and often baked cakes for tea – jam sponge, gingerbread, fruitcake – and always special cakes for our birthdays. But best of all was the apple turnover she made on autumn evenings, with cooking apples from the trees in the orchard. I would sit at the kitchen counter, as the world outside slipped away in the gathering darkness, peeling and slicing the apples, while she made the pastry and we chatted about all the important events of the day.

'Mrs Guinea Pig is going to have more babies,' I told her.

'Oh no, how many do we have already?'

'It's hard to tell because so many of them have escaped from their cage, but I think there are nearly forty.'

'We should try and catch some of them and sell them,' she said.

'Oh, but how many people can say they have a herd of wild guinea pigs living in their garden?' I protested.

'How many people would want to?' she replied, laughing.

When the pastry was ready she rolled it out into a large rectangle, placed the sliced apples on one half, folded the other over the top, joined the edges together and baked it. That was it, no spices, no sugar, no raisins, no nothing, yet out it would come, twenty long minutes later, the apple soft and melting and exquisitely tart against the crisp, buttery pastry. It was soooooo delicious and I have eaten my way around the world, tasting every apple pie, tart, puff, crumble and turnover that has crossed my path, in search of just one more taste of it. A taste that will transport me back to childhood and into the presence of my mother's love.

She was also brilliant at making things: she made me skirts and pinafore dresses and knitted hot-water-bottle covers and woolly hats for us all. These were identical in shape, thick and squashy like a cottage loaf and just as warm, as if they too had been pulled straight out of the oven. Mine was made from fluffy red mohair and I finally persuaded her to knit me a jumper from the same wool. In the evenings, we clustered around the fire in the sitting room, cats on laps and dogs sprawled out in front of the hearth. While we watched lions and other exotic wildlife prowl across the TV screen, Tate knitted, a slim current of red flowing through her fingers and gradually forming into my very own, very precious, red sweater.

She liked funny words and silly voices and we all made up names and phrases and jokes to share with each other, our own private currency. That was how she came to be called Tate. When I was about thirteen Bonnie made friends with three men who were visiting the Isle of Wight from Australia to study farming. They were charming, handsome and larger than life. They soon became regular visitors and often arrived in the early evening when Tate was standing at the sink peeling potatoes for dinner. Gathering together like a barber-shop trio, they would serenade her with a bawdy Australian song called 'Potato-Peeler Sheila'. Apparently women in Australia are often referred to as 'sheilas', but Sheelagh also happened to be my mother's name. Soon they had shortened potato to

Tate. 'G'd evening, Tate,' they'd say as they came in the door, 'how are ya?' The name stuck.

Soon I stopped calling her Mum and started calling her Tate too. It helped in a way. 'Tate' made her special and it seemed to give her a little more space than 'Mum', a little more permission to be who she was. The rules and expectations that applied to Mum didn't apply to Tate. A mum would have been constant, dependable, a safe and reassuring ally. Tate was, well, what she was – funny, charming, loving, tempestuous and terrifying.

Those eyebrows of hers were not menacing for nothing and if the first weapon in her arsenal was charm, the second was fury. She was extremely volatile and unpredictable and lived life on a hair trigger, so that it was impossible to know what kind of mood she would be in from one moment to the next or when she would erupt into rage. There were no rules or reliable warning signs and at times I seriously wondered if she was crazy. Maybe she was just exhausted and frustrated, ground down by the chores and responsibilities of being a wife and mother. Maybe she was deeply unhappy. Or maybe she mothered us the only way she knew how, the way she herself had been mothered. Whatever the cause, the changes in her temperament were devastating.

I remember lying in bed one night when I was six years old. A small pool of light shone out across my pillow from my night light, the rest of my room was dark, but I knew exactly what it looked like. There was pale pastel-striped wallpaper on the walls and pretty blue-and-white flowered curtains, which Tate had made, hung at the window.

Mobiles dangled from the ceiling with fish and butter-flies and witches flying on broomsticks, wearing neat little skirts and headscarves of brightly coloured felt. In one corner there was a pile of teddies all snuggled together and next to them dolls lay in prams and little wooden beds, tucked up safe and cosily under miniature sheets and blankets.

Everything was as it should be, except that downstairs I could hear my parents fighting and instead of drifting happily off to sleep, I lay rigid with terror, every fibre of my body stretched taut, every nerve jangling, my ears straining to catch every word. 'I hate you!' Tate shouted. 'You've ruined my life. I wish I'd never married you. I wish I'd never set eyes on you . . .' My father's voice was quieter and more controlled and I couldn't make out his words, but I could hear his voice surge with hurt and anger in response.

I was worried the fight was my fault, which was why I desperately wanted to hear, so I could find out what I had done wrong and make sure I didn't do it again. I was so terrified of provoking a row that I tried always to be on my best behaviour and I learnt to police my every word and action in case it contained some unintended detonating mechanism. But I still made mistakes and I was forever trying to be more careful.

The fight concluded with my mother walking out of the house and slamming the door behind her. My father followed and I heard more shouting outside and then the sound of a car starting. As I listened to her drive off into the night, I thought, That's it, she's gone, I have to look after myself from now on, there is no one I can trust.

Sometime later that night my mother came back. She always did come back, but that was not the point. The point was that one day she might not. This was my greatest fear: that one day there would be a final row and she would leave for ever. As there was frequent fighting – and not just between Dad and Tate – I lived on constant red alert, my whole body tense and my stomach in knots. For even when things appeared to be fine, when the picnic was going smoothly and the skies were clear, thunderclouds could form in an instant and all hell would break loose.

A quiet morning out in the stable yard, for instance, could suddenly turn into a war zone. On one occasion I remember hiding behind a stable door as Tate and Bonnie chased each other around the yard, hitting each other with pitchforks. It was like watching a Tom and Jerry cartoon. Except this wasn't a cartoon, it was my mother and sister caught up in a storm of blows, so angry and out of control they seemed capable of killing each other.

We had so much that was wonderful, so much that we shared and did together, so much that was done on my behalf and yet for me fear tainted everything – every holiday, every Christmas, every birthday, every outing, every meal, every moment. And it was not just frightening, it was heartbreaking. More than anything else I wanted us all to love each other, to be kind and happy, and I felt sure this was possible. Sure that love was the antidote to the cycle of anger and hurt in which we lived.

When I was about eight, I was in the kitchen with my parents when some minor incident sparked into another blazing row.

'That's it!' my mother screamed. 'I've had it. I can't bear to go on living like this any longer.' Insults and accusations quickly followed, words slicing through the air as sharp as knives.

'Stop, stop!' I cried, trying to step in between them.

'Please stop. Please don't say such awful things!'

Tate pushed me aside, my pleas lost amidst the buffeting winds of anger and recrimination. So I stepped back and looked at my parents, at their faces twisted with rage, wondering why did they do this?

As I stood there, scared and bewildered, I suddenly felt myself surrounded by the presence of Love. My parents' voices faded momentarily into the background as the feeling washed over me. Love – unconditional, unmistakable, enveloping me, filling me with hope and comfort. Deep within me my soul responded and I was filled with the certainty that it was possible to live another way and that way was Love. In that moment I vowed that no matter what it took I would learn how. It was a vow I would come to renew in many different forms.

Looking back I can see this experience was important on many levels. It was the first time I experienced the existence and power of unconditional Divine Love. It was the first time I was consciously aware of the presence of my soul – the place of inner knowing and wisdom that stirred within me. Just as importantly it was the first time I realized that we have a choice about how we live. That we can choose to act from love and kindness rather than from fear and anger.

But then, in spite of all my efforts to be good and loving, the thing I most dreaded had come true: I had made a mistake and Tate had gone. Permanently.

I tried as best I could to fill the hole she had left, especially for my father and brother. The shopping and cooking were just one way I could take care of them and in the beginning I was glad to do it; glad to do anything that helped appease the guilt I felt. But after a few months it became a terrible strain. The cooking itself wasn't the problem; what I found hardest was deciding day after day what to cook. If I asked Dad or Geoff what they wanted, they just said, 'Cook whatever you like.' Which was no help. I didn't care if I ever ate again. I was only doing it to please them and how was I supposed to do that if they wouldn't tell me?

But I didn't want to let the strain show so I just went on pretending, pretending, pretending to be fine. I'd had so many years of practice that it came easily enough and I managed to convince everybody that I really was OK – even myself. After all 'life goes on', they say. The bizarre thing was life did go on. One month became two months, two months became three months. And there were times I spent with my friends when I dropped out of my worries and guilt and back into life, laughing and acting just like any other teenager. There were also times when family friends came over for dinner and we gathered around the kitchen table and chatted and laughed just as before, although now our friends often brought their friends with them. Specifically, single women for my father to meet.

I hated the prospect of my father dating another woman – even though it was clearly inevitable. To me it seemed like a complete betrayal of Tate. She was barely dead and he was already looking for a replacement. Despite a conversation in which he explained that of course he loved Tate, but he was lonely and wanted to start a new life, I had no tolerance for it. I felt angry and resentful, although once again I was silenced by guilt and the thought that if I hadn't killed her, none of this would be happening.

I remember one woman in particular, who came for lunch. She was slightly plump, with grey bobbed hair and a kind face. 'Where does your strength come from?' she asked me, completely out of the blue.

We were standing together by the kitchen sink clearing up dishes and I looked at her in surprise, taking in the powdery lines of her face and the directness of her gaze. It was true I did feel strong, but I was amazed that anyone else had noticed. I pointed to my stomach. 'In here,' I said, shrugging. 'I don't know what it is or where it comes from, I just feel it.'

'It's God,' she said.

Luckily I had just put down the pile of plates I was carrying, otherwise I would have dropped the lot. My expression changed from surprise to utter incredulousness and I stared at her for a moment, before mumbling, 'Oh.'

God was never mentioned in our house, except in tones of the utmost derision. From as early as I can remember I accepted my father's opinion that God – an old man in the sky with a beard – was ridiculous. My father was a classic intellectual. He was immensely knowledgeable on just about everything from Plato to Samuel Beckett, via big-band jazz and the Impressionist painters. He was also sceptical and rational to the core and he insisted that life was 'random and meaningless' and that we had appeared in a mechnical universe by accident alone.

Religion was therefore, by his definition, a complete sham and corrupt to boot. And there were only two types of people who believed in God. The weak and feeble-minded, who needed a crutch to help them get through the ordeal of life. Or those who suffered from an appalling arrogance and tried to deify themselves, by casting God in their own image. My father had total contempt for both categories and I was quite certain I didn't want to fall into either one, so I became an ardent champion of his opinions.

The trouble was, in order to avoid my father's scorn I had to deny and hide what I did feel. Like many children I was full of a nascent spiritual curiosity and hunger. In Hinduism it is said that in the womb babies sing a song to God: 'Oh God, please help me remember who I truly am.' And that on being born the baby's first cry means: 'Oh God, help me, I am forgetting.' In other words it is part of the human experience to forget that the true source of our being is the great mystery we call God. As a result, instead of knowing that we are part of God, we identify with our body, mind and ego and come to believe that we are separate and alone, to the point where we often deny that the spiritual realm exists at all. And out of that tiny mistake in identity everything else arises – all the fears, problems and dramas of our lives and our world.

Yet Hinduism and other spiritual traditions tell us that even though we forget, the truth is still within us. And that we are born with the longing to reconnect with our source and remember who we really are, just as the salmon is born with the longing to return to the place of its birth. As a young child I was full of such longing, but in the face of my father's scorn, I became ashamed of it, dismissing my spiritual hunger as something foolish and stupid, and learning instead to pride myself upon my ability to be logical and rational.

But if my father helped reinforce the split between the rational and the spiritual, and between my ego and my soul, my religious education failed utterly to restore it or give me any insight into the true nature of God. Despite my father's aversion to religion, at thirteen I was sent to a Church of England boarding school, because it was the best school on the island, where I was forced to attend chapel. Nothing the vicar said made any sense to me. He droned on day after day, intoning earnestly about repentance and eternal life. And his version of God – a judgemental, heavenly Father who created the world and gave his only begotten son to save us from sin – seemed just as absurd as the 'old man' my father fulminated against.

However, a year later, longing to be part of something, I decided to get confirmed. There was a stunned silence at the dinner table when I finally plucked up the courage to tell Dad. He put down his knife and fork, his face a picture of utter astonishment. 'Well, if you want to,' he said at last, 'there is nothing I can do to stop you. But you know I think it's a load of complete and utter nonsense.' He resumed eating gloomily, with the air of one whose pet project had suddenly gone disappointingly wrong.

The whole event was completely anticlimactic. After the ceremony was over, among all the proud parents, Dad was the only one who stood there dismayed and disbelieving. I was disappointed too for there had been no moment of revelation, no feeling of connecting with something sacred and profound as I stood at the altar. I obediently repeated the words pledging myself to the Church, but they were just words, as empty of meaning for me as the prayers I was forced to say every day in chapel.

Rather than teaching me how to connect with the source of my being, I was left feeling more alone and adrift than ever, and I turned to my rational mind instead.

Dad is right, I thought bitterly, this is all complete rubbish; and I rejected the idea of God completely. At fifteen I pronounced myself an atheist and refused to attend any more religious education classes. Not that my spiritual hunger went away of course, it simply went under another name – the longing for happiness.

From that point on I assumed my dealings with God were over and I didn't ever think about it, unless a 'believer', like the woman who came to lunch, happened to stumble across my path. Had she been my age, I would have teased her mercilessly; as it was I looked away from her in embarrassment and began putting plates into the dishwasher. She helped for a few minutes and then tactfully made a retreat back to the table. Well that rules you out, I thought as I watched her walk away: one mention of God and Dad will run a mile.

The days grew shorter and colder as the year wheeled by. Everything in the house was still exactly as it had been when Tate was there. Her gumboots were in the boot room, her coats hung on the rack, her clothes were in the linen cupboard, her bathroom cabinet still contained her favourite pale-blue eyeshadow and the little pot of wax that she used to remove the fine, dark hairs from her upper lip. On several occasions Dad alluded to the time when we would 'sort through her things', but I pushed it out of my mind, because it was another thing I couldn't bear to think about.

At the end of October, nearly four months after the accident, the fateful day arrived and Bon came to stay for the weekend to help. To me, this dismantling of my mother's life, piece by piece, was not just an admission that she was really dead, it was also a process of removing the evidence of her existence from the house and our lives. It was not about letting go or setting Tate free; we were erasing her and getting rid of belongings that were a painful reminder of something that we couldn't talk about or deal with in any way. For I was by no means the only one unable to speak about my feelings or grieve for her death. As we unloaded her things from cupboards and wardrobes the wrench of separation was almost audible, like the rip of the cooled wax from the soft skin of her face.

We started with the drawers. Here were piles of nylon stockings, a pair of elbow-length gold lamé gloves, a little black suede evening bag emblazoned with the Royal Air Force crest, given to her by a wartime admirer. I looked inside and found what seemed to be a tiny gold pen, but instead of a nib, the end unfurled like the spines of a miniature umbrella.

'What's this?' I asked Dad.

'It's a swizzle stick,' he replied. 'For taking the bubbles out of champagne.'

My mother and a swizzle stick? I felt the all too familiar surge of sadness stirring in my chest – there was so much about her I didn't know. So much I would never know.

From the drawers we worked our way through the racks of clothes. Here were her long, flowing, multicoloured Yuki dresses. The salmon-pink chiffon dress with matching coat that was her wedding outfit. Even her dreaded chicken chasers – a pair of raggedy old blue polyester ski-pants she wore to feed her chickens – tugged at my heart-strings. On this particular subject Dad, Bon, Geoff and I were united: we hated those trousers and were vociferous in telling her so. Although in truth, perhaps it was the chickens we hated, because Tate seemed to love them so much more than us.

Bon and I handed things backwards and forwards to each other. 'What shall we do with this?'

'I don't know. Do you want it?'

'No. Should we give it away?'

Slowly, painfully, the mound of clothes on the floor grew like a pile of peelings, potato peelings, shaved away from memory.

At the end of the day we reached her bedroom and the dressing table where she kept her jewellery. We were tired and the last of a cold, wintry afternoon light filtered through the bedroom window. Tenderly we opened the boxes, pulling back folds of ageing tissue paper to reveal broken strands of beads, several watches that had long stopped ticking, a garnet ring and then another, bought to replace the first one, which had been lost and found again a year later, hidden in a box of Christmas wrapping paper.

At the back of the drawer was a small, tatty, square box. I picked it up, opened it and gasped. Inside was a pair of crystal earrings – a single large drop, hanging from a much smaller crystal stud. They were beautiful, but that wasn't why I gasped; it was because I had felt a current of energy pass through my body as I held them. They glittered and sparkled with a life of their own. Her life-force, I thought to myself, still tingling: she is in these earrings. I said nothing and offered them to Bon.

'No, you have them,' she answered. 'They should belong to you.'

Somehow we lurched on and made it through all the dreaded 'firsts' without Tate. The first Christmas, Dad's first birthday, my first birthday, her first birthday. We barely ever talked about her. It was so difficult to even mention her name that we didn't share memories or stories and we certainly never confessed to each other how much we missed her or how empty life was without her. We might have removed her things, but she remained, wandering among us like Banquo's ghost. Instead of acknowledging her, we politely stepped around her and got on with our lives as best we could.

At Christmas Bonnie announced she was getting married. By the spring everything was in full production for the wedding in May and I was caught up in a flurry of dress designers, caterers and flower-arrangers. Even without Tate it was a lovely day. The church was full of flowers and our elderly vicar managed to remember the names of both Bonnie and her husband Oliver. Back home the cherry trees danced in a sea of white blossoms and waiters stood to attention holding trays of champagne and canapés.

My brother's best friend, Thomas, supervised the parking dressed in a gorilla outfit, and even the children found ways to entertain themselves. 'Mummy! Mummy!' I heard one little girl say, as she tugged at her mother's pale-yellow silk dress with dark, sticky fingers. 'He's eaten over twenty chocolate éclairs!' I looked to see who on earth she could be talking about and there at the end of her pointing finger was our dog Cromwell, adorable and greedy as only a Labrador can be.

In July I sat my A level exams. I was taking three subjects – English Literature, Geography and Economics. I had already given up any attempt to study Economics because it was far too boring, but I couldn't muster any enthusiasm for the other subjects either. I looked through my Geography textbook as I lay in the bath on the morning of the exam and that was my only concession to revision. Fortunately there were enough questions that I could answer and I finished the paper feeling pretty confident that I had at least passed.

The English exam was another matter. It wasn't that I hadn't read the books. Or that I couldn't answer the questions. It was the poem they included for the comprehension section of the exam: 'Vergissmeinnicht, 1943' by the Second World War poet Keith Douglas. In it Douglas describes crossing back over the nightmare ground of a battlefield. He finds the body of a German soldier he fought against, and lying beside the body in the spoil of the gunpit, a photograph of the German's girlfriend upon which she has written: 'Steffi. Vergissmeinnicht.'

Forget Me Not. As I read those words something in me crumbled. What I had been unable to share with anyone I confessed to an empty page and my grief poured out. When the teacher announced the exam was over, I stopped writing, looked up and was amazed to find myself still in the examination hall. It was like coming out of a trance and I realized that I had completely screwed up the exam. I imagined the examiner reading my paper and sadly giving me zero marks for that section, because you don't get marks for reducing the examiner to tears, you get marks for analysing style and technique and I had neglected to do that.

Dad was waiting eagerly for me at home. I had applied to Goldsmiths College, London University to study English Literature and my grade for this exam was critical in determining whether I would be admitted.

'How did it go?' he asked, the moment I stepped in the door.

'Not too well,' I answered reluctantly.

He waited for an explanation, but I couldn't possibly tell him what had happened. So I simply shrugged my shoulders and turned away. His disappointment was obvious, but I felt nothing because by that time I was so depressed and exhausted I didn't care.

'Oh, well,' my father went on, 'I am sure you did your best and we'll know soon enough. When do the results come through?' His words, intended I am sure to comfort me, only cut deeper. All my life I had believed that his love was conditional on my being brilliant, and I had failed his expectations yet again.

'Not for at least six weeks,' I replied automatically. 'I should get a letter sometime in the middle of August.'

August. It seemed like an eternity away. The summer term finished and without the distraction of school, time slowed to an unbearable crawl and I had nothing to shield me from the growing terror I felt inside. I had practically stopped eating, my feeling of inner strength had worn down to nothing, and it took every remaining ounce of effort and will-power just to make it through each day. I spent most of my time lying motionless in the sun by our swimming pool, pretending that I wanted a suntan. In reality I was incapable of doing anything else.

Geoff came home from work each day and joined me outside. He would swim and then lie down in the sun beside me to dry. 'Ah, it's all right for some – living the life of luxury,' he'd say, 'while the rest of us have to work for a living.' When that failed to get a response, he would try another tack. 'Don't you get bored doing nothing all day?'

I could only shake my head in reply, because there were no words to explain how desperate I felt.

It was almost a year since Tate's death and my own longing to be dead grew stronger every day. I had a recurring vision of myself lying right on the edge of a high cliff. I was clinging to a piece of rope that was staked to the ground a short distance away. It was all that stopped me from falling, but it was of little comfort, for every day the stake shifted closer to the edge. I didn't fully understand what was happening to me, but I knew I was near breaking point and I wondered if I was going mad.

After a week of days filled with dark despair I couldn't bear it any more and I decided to commit suicide. With more determination than I had felt in ages, I walked upstairs to the bathroom, locked the door and emptied the contents of the medicine cupboard into my lap – sleeping pills, aspirin and everything else I could find. But I couldn't take them. I have already caused everyone enough pain, I thought to myself, as I rearranged the bottles on the shelf and dragged myself back out to the sun.

Then a miracle happened.

3. A Glimpse of Freedom

It was traditional for the members of my family to go and visit our cousins, Joan and Steve Prince, at their summer cabin in the Cascade Mountains in Oregon as a reward for finishing A levels. Now it was my turn and my ticket was booked for the end of July. When I got off the plane I found it had not only taken me to another country, it had taken me to another world.

Joan was my godmother and my father's first cousin. They had grown up together with their various brothers and sisters in the same house in England. During the Second World War, Joan met Steve, an American Red Cross ambulance driver, they fell in love, and after the war was over they married and she went to live in America with him. I loved Joan from the first time I remember meeting her, when I was four or five years old. She was so kind and gentle and I immediately felt safe with her. Nothing had changed in the intervening years and when I arrived at the airport, she and Steve were both there to meet me, warm and welcoming, with smiling faces and friendly hugs.

Outside it was a hot, clear day, with a bright, bright blue sky. I looked around me as we drove through Portland, eager to know this new place, and I was struck by the style of America – the vibrantly coloured clothes people wore, the orderly, geometric layout of the city, the enormous cars that cruised down the road like boats, and the shape of the old pick-up trucks, so curved and generous. It was all so different from anything I had ever seen before. Britain, especially the Isle of Wight, with its regulation green Barbour waterproof jackets and wellington boots, seemed extremely dull and dowdy by comparison.

Then there were the health-food stores. We stopped at one called Nature's as we drove out of Portland. At first I thought, Oh what a bore, I've only just arrived and we have to go grocery shopping, and the dismal little super-market that I went to every week on the island, with its limp lettuces and floury potatoes, flashed before my eyes. Maybe I'll be able to stay in the car, I hoped.

But Steve said, 'Why don't you come in and choose what you want to eat for breakfast.'

Reluctantly, I followed them, only to stop with amaze-ment just inside the front door. A huge display of veget-ables and fruit met my eyes – fresh corn; yellow squash; snow peas; great big glossy purple aubergines; huge, deep-red cherries; pineapples and mangoes. Everything so fresh and alive and organic – whatever that meant.

The smell of freshly baked bread wafted through the air and I followed my nose deeper into the store, like one drawn into paradise by some mysterious and seduc-tive perfume. There was an entire row of bulk bins full of dried fruits, nuts, grains and beans. The shelves and coolers were stocked with an astonishing variety of produce, from fresh salsa and guacamole to blue corn chips and dried papaya, and I wandered along the aisles in a daze marvelling at all the things I had never even heard of. Finally Steve came to find me. 'We've got bread, cereal, milk and tea,' he said. 'Is there anything else you would like?'

'No. Yes. Everything!' I said, my hands stretched out in wonder.

'Come on,' he replied smiling. 'This is just the beginning.'

We drove to their cabin in the mountains, nestled amid a chain of peaks with romantic names like Broken Top and Three Fingered Jack. The cabin was a simple wooden building, built on the banks of the Metolius River by Steve's grandfather in the 1930s. It was tucked in under ponderosa pine trees, stretching a hundred feet and more up into the sky. Across the yard on the left-hand side there was a little guest cabin where I stayed and on the right a storage barn. A small stretch of lawn and the tangle of plants and wild flowers on the river bank were all that separated the buildings from the river itself: clear, icy water, glistening and rippling, murmuring its soft, ancient song.

The following morning we ate breakfast outside. The air was still cool, but the sun filtered through the trees, creating pools of rich, warm light, and Steve had expertly positioned the table so that its white cloth gleamed in the sunshine. There were glasses of freshly squeezed orange juice, a bowl of fruit, natural yoghurt, several types of cereal and a basket of toast made from delicious granary bread, thick and warm and nutty.

I could hardly wait to taste it. As I sank my teeth into my first slice I felt as if the world had turned from black and white to colour. Suddenly I was awake to the sheer pleasure of eating, of sitting outside in the morning sun, surrounded by the trees and the murmur of the river. Everything seemed new, full of magic and beauty, as if I was seeing, tasting, feeling for the first time, and I was flooded with the simple joy of being alive.

The nightmare of guilt and despair I had been living in England fled to the back of my mind, banished by the bright mountain light and the endless blue skies. No one mentioned Tate's death, until one day, after I had been there for a week or so, Joan said, 'I am so sorry about the accident.' We were hanging up laundry on the line outside and she paused with a handful of socks. 'I couldn't believe it when I heard what had happened. I have been so worried for you – it must have been absolutely awful.'

'Yes,' I replied, blankly, 'it was.'

Even though I couldn't talk about it, just being away from the whole thing for a few weeks was an immense relief. It gave me time to replenish my spirits and remember why it was actually a good thing to be alive. We spent our days outside, rafting down the river in inflatable kayaks, canoeing and swimming in the lakes and hiking in the mountains. At first I didn't really appreciate the point of hiking. The long uphill climbs seemed like unnecessary hard work and not nearly as much fun as canoeing or rafting. Then one day as I was grumpily puffing my way uphill I glanced over at Joan. She was looking out over the valley, but she turned towards me smiling, her face alive with delight and joy, as her bright blue eyes met mine. Her look was an invitation, an initiation, for it touched me like a spark, setting me ablaze with the same joy. In that moment my attention switched. Instead of being caught in my own little world, I was instantly aware of what was happening all around me – a leaf caught in a beam of golden light, the subtle colours of the rocks and stones, the fragrance of the pine trees warmed by the sun and the way the view unfolded before me step by step. It was all so outrageously beautiful. Lakes shimmered in the valleys below us, ringed with dark pine trees that swept up the mountainsides, finally giving way to jagged peaks, capped with snow. I felt a surge of energy and vitality, my heart grew big, filling my chest, and suddenly it didn't matter that the climb was steep or that my legs ached. All that mattered was experiencing this vast, unbounded feeling of joy.

I had felt glimmers of this joy before, especially when I rode over the downs at home. My pony and I would gallop right up on to the top and pause for a moment to take in the view. From that spot the island narrowed to a point on the horizon and the ocean swept in on either side. Fields rolled away in a lacework of hedges and lanes, with farms dotted here and there and villages nestled into the folds of the land. Beyond it all was the vast, empty sky.

Even then I sensed a presence, an energy that coursed through the land, whipping up our excitement like the wind. While my pony tossed his head, eager to gallop on down the other side, my soul, curled up deep inside me like an animal in hibernation, would flutter and stir, stretching and opening for a wide amazing moment, before it settled down again, waiting patiently for its time to come. In those moments I gazed out and felt myself fill with a deep sense of love and awe and an inexpressible hope for all that life might contain.

Then the feeling would pass, fleeting and tantalizing, leaving me with a yearning for something I could not explain. Because I had rejected the whole idea of God, it never even crossed my mind that God might have something to do with the mystery I sensed, or the longing I felt or the questions that so fascinated me: Who are we? Where do we come from? And what is our purpose here? I didn't talk to my family about any of these things. Partly to protect myself from the ridicule of my brother and father. Partly because I was aware that the experiences I had on the downs made me different in some way and that was definitely not a good thing to be.

The feeling of being different was a dreadful, shameful secret that I carried with me constantly. I tried to keep it hidden at all costs, but it bothered me so much that one day when I was about twelve, in a moment of desperate vulnerability, I confessed to Tate that I was worried I didn't fit in. I wanted her to reassure me. To say we are all unique and that this is what makes each person so special. In other words to let me know that it was OK to be me. We all need this as children. In order to develop a healthy sense of self we need to know that we are precious and lovable just the way we are.

Instead she looked at me for a moment and said, 'Well, you are a bit of an oddball.' Her words knocked the breath out of me and I managed to stay vertical long enough to stagger upstairs to my room, where I collapsed on my bed, haemorrhaging self-esteem. Now I knew there was no hope, no way I could ever be normal or good enough, because even my own mother thought I was 'an oddball'!

Except that I couldn't give up hope, because to give up the hope of fitting in was to give up the hope of being really loved and to give up the hope of being really loved was to give up the desire to live. I longed for love. I needed it to survive, just as much as I needed food or oxygen. It was equally important to have my love accepted and received in return. And that didn't happen. If I won a riding competition or passed an exam or said something clever – then for a brief moment I would bask in the glow of love and approval. But it soon faded, leaving me more certain than ever that love was a prize, hanging like a sweet ripe peach just out of my reach.

So I went on existing largely due to my enduring hope that one day I might be able to do better, and I tried harder and harder to win my family's love. Over time, like an actor playing a part, I developed a version of myself that I hoped would be more lovable than the real me. Until I ended up living a double life, with my real thoughts, feelings, dreams, likes and dislikes hidden from view.

Unfortunately, the more I tried to fit in and please, the more unsatisfying the love and approval I did receive became, because I knew it wasn't given to the real me – just to the 'little miss nice' version of myself I had become. I lived in dread of being found out, of being revealed as an impostor living inside my own skin. And the greater the gap between the real me and the way I appeared to be, the more I hated my real self, because I believed 'I' was the obstacle to receiving the love I so desperately wanted.

In psychology this process of creating an acceptable version of ourselves is known as 'developing a persona' and we all do it to some extent, coerced by the need for love and approval to conform to our family's definition of how we are allowed to be. And it can cripple our entire lives, because we allow this limited sense of self to determine all the decisions and choices we make, and it is difficult to let it go because we assume that our family is right and therefore expect the whole world to judge us in the same way. Yet with the Princes I felt loved and accepted unconditionally. Steve and Joan had no preconceived ideas about who I was or how I was supposed to be. And for a few brief weeks, in the face of that love, I began to feel that maybe, just maybe, it was actually OK to be the very thing I had spent my whole life learning how not to be – me.

It was fascinating talking to my cousins, Susie, William and Jonathon. Their values and attitudes about life, money, career and class were completely different from anything I had experienced. They seemed so relaxed and happy and comfortable with themselves, and they didn't appear at all anxious about saying or doing the right thing. None of the things that were so important in England – like speaking with the correct accent or how you held your knife and fork or where you went to school – made the slightest bit of difference to them. Suddenly I could see English culture from the outside and I realized how tightly bound it was by conventions and class.

'Do you have any idea how lucky you are?' I asked William one day. 'Or how much freedom you have?' I looked at him in his cut-off jeans and pink long-sleeved collarless cotton shirt. 'You can wear whatever you want and no one judges you. You can do what you like, say how you feel and not risk becoming a social outcast, because you aren't trapped in a class system.'

'That's true here and in a few other parts of America,' he agreed. 'But certainly not everywhere – there are plenty of places where people would judge me for these clothes. But you're right: here it is different. So to answer your question, yes, I do realize that I am lucky, because I have found places to live where I can be myself.'

The more time I spent with my cousins the more I

could see that not only had I been shaped by my family, I had also been moulded by the larger culture in which I grew up. Under the influence of this twofold conditioning process, I had built up in my mind a whole set of patterns, beliefs, expectations and assumptions about life, which were as rigid and confining as the walls of any prison. These patterns and beliefs had become my reality and the world – the world of infinite possibility – had become fixed and narrowed to an endless repetition of what was already known. Yet here were my cousins, living evidence that my version of reality was not the definitive reality at all.

I was lying on a swing chair one afternoon looking out over the river, feeling trapped and frustrated by my situation, when it dawned on me that I didn't have to follow the path that had been laid out for me. Instead I could take responsibility for my life, for my decisions and choices. Like so many insights, the idea emerged out of the stillness and silence to tap me on the shoulder, as if it had been waiting patiently for years to present itself for my consideration. My mind somersaulted. I felt a surge of hope and excitement as my life opened up, offering itself to me, ripe with potential. For in seeing that there was another way to live, all things became possible and I was able to consciously ask myself for the first time: What kind of life do I want?

I wanted to be happy, I knew that much. I wanted to be the real me. I wanted truth and love and freedom. I didn't know what that would look like or how to find it, but I promised myself that I would learn, little realizing the magnitude of the commitment I was making.

★

On a psychological level, freeing ourselves from our persona and conditioning in order to create a healthy and authentic personality is known as individuation and it is an important process in its own right. But from a spiritual perspective, individuation is part of a much greater process of becoming free and whole, in which we move beyond our ego and personality altogether to discover the source of our being or true nature – the universal consciousness or energy of which we are each a unique expression.

This greater process of awakening or self-realization has been recognized by spiritual traditions for thousands of years. In ancient Greece it was summed up by the maxim 'Know Thyself', which was inscribed above the gateway to the Oracle at Delphi. In the Indian tradition of Advaita Vedanta, the teacher, Ramana Maharshi, taught his students to ask themselves the question 'Who am I?' so they could let go of the little self of ego, mind and body in order to connect with the indwelling presence of that which is 'infinite, divine, eternal'.

Regardless of the spiritual tradition, the ability to wake up and discover who we really are as opposed to who we think we are is seen as a natural part of being human and the ultimate purpose in life. Unfortunately, given Western society's fixation on the rational and the material, it is no longer very natural for us. This is the problem and challenge of living in a culture that denies and diminishes the spiritual dimension of life. But our cultural blindness doesn't mean our true nature has changed – it is still there, as it will always be there, waiting for us to discover it.

This lack of understanding was part of my problem and challenge too. At the age of eighteen nothing in my upbringing or education had prepared me to think about my true nature or my potential as a human being. Nor to consider that life might be a spiritual journey. Yet without realizing it, at least not consciously, I had embarked upon the path of self-realization simply because I wanted to be free, and it turns out that longing is enough to carry us home, back to our source — to the invisible presence that is God.

So as I got ready to leave Oregon, I had no idea what I had signed up for or how to do it. But fortunately we don't need to know how, any more than a rose bush needs to know how to grow a rose. But we do need to be willing to try. We have to take responsibility for our lives. We have to start paying attention to what is happening and why. Above all we need to follow our longing for happiness, truth and freedom. If we can do that, then life — the great teacher — will send us all the experiences and lessons we need to heal and grow. One step at a time.

When I got back to England everything was waiting for me just as I had left it. My guilt, my fear and my A level results. I failed to get the B I needed in English to qualify for my place at university. Although I hadn't expected any better, I was still disappointed and the expansive, hope-filled vista of my future life deflated in front of my very eyes. Then my determination kicked in. OK, I thought, I will just have to retake my English exam. I couldn't face going back to my old school on the island, so I persuaded Dad to send me to a college in Winchester for people who were retaking exams. Bonnie and Oliver lived nearby, in a cottage on an island in the middle of a river, and they invited me to come and stay with them. As I carried my bags over the little wooden bridge and upstairs to my new room, I felt a deep sense of relief and gratitude.

It was September, and when I woke in the mornings bright autumn sunshine poured in through the open curtains. I lay snuggled up in bed, listening to the river rippling past my window, to the cheerful sounds of Bonnie and Oliver downstairs making breakfast and to the dogs – two Jack Russell terriers – who raced out to greet the day barking. I too savoured each new day. Oregon already seemed a long way away, but I had glimpsed what was possible: now I had to translate that into action. With the help of my new English teacher and Bonnie's encouragement I retook my exam and got a B.

4. Walking Wounded

On my first day at Goldsmiths I followed signs through a maze of corridors to the English Department meeting room. About fifty chairs were scattered around, with a handful of people already sitting in them. I chose a seat by the window and gradually the room began to fill up with my fellow students.

'I'm Alys,' said a woman in her late twenties, plonking herself down in a chair next to me. She had a huge pile of orange curly hair stacked up on top of her head and a goofy, lopsided smile. 'I used to be a social worker,' she went on, 'until I thought, Sod that for a laugh, it's time to try something different.'

I liked her immediately.

'So why are you here?' she asked.

Our conversation was suddenly interrupted by my intuition. 'The man you are going to fall in love with has just walked in,' it said. Although I quite often had an intuitive feeling about things, it was rare to get such a clear message and I spun around in my seat away from Alys in astonishment, to see who had walked in the door. And there he was. A tall young man, with dark-brown hair that curled deliciously down over his forehead, grey eyes, broad cheekbones and a smile that sparkled across his face like sunshine on water. 'You won't spend your whole life together,' my intuition added, 'but you will love each other very much.' He settled down in a chair and looked up.

My heart was pounding and I quickly looked away, too surprised to catch his eye.

The first few weeks at college flashed by as all the unknown elements of my new life became familiar. I learnt exactly what time I had to get out of bed to be in class by 9 a.m. And the quickest way through the labyrinth of corridors – because I never did make it out of bed quite on time. I learnt which professors were the most interesting and who out of my fifty fellow English students I wanted to be friends with. Including Ben. I saw him most days, but I felt so shy I couldn't talk to him. In fact I could barely meet his eye, despite the fact that we sat next to each other once a week in a class on William Blake. Don't ask me about Blake's poetry, because I have no idea what we were taught. I was too fascinated by the arcs of electricity that jumped between Ben's body and mine to think about anything else.

I woke up each morning with a sense of satisfaction and excitement at my new life. I could be whoever I wanted to be, I thought to myself gleefully, as I walked along the corridors from one class to the next. Do whatever I wanted to do, say whatever I wanted to say. But to my disappointment I discovered that I couldn't. I had changed my outer environment, but my inner environment remained the same. You can't just run away, I realized, as I stared out of the window during a class on Anglo-Saxon literature, because until you sort out your problems you carry them with you wherever you go.

So although I came across as bright, independent, capable and charming, inside I was still riddled by self-doubt. The brief, wondrous feeling I had in Oregon that it might actually be OK to be me had evaporated like a wisp of a dream as soon as I got back to England, leaving me trapped once again in the vice-like grip of the belief that I was not good enough. I found it difficult to share my ideas in class, because I was terrified that people would think what I said was wrong or stupid. And while my classmates sat in the student coffee bar, laughing and chatting with apparent ease, I sat with them feeling awkward and paralysed, convinced that I didn't fit in because I wasn't smart enough or funny enough or beautiful enough or cool enough. Not enough, not enough, not enough.

Goldsmiths was in an area called New Cross, one of the poorest and noisiest parts of London. The college itself was an imposing white building with a large porticoed front door, a vestige of grander and more prosperous days. Now blocks of desolate concrete high-rise council flats loomed on the horizon. Cars and lorries roared by belching exhaust fumes. Litter swirled in their wake – brightly coloured plastic chocolate wrappers and greasy paper bags stained by last night's fish and chips. Tabloid newspapers, tossed aside at the bus stop, unfurled and flapped up into the sky. The bare-breasted pin-up girls fluttered back down to earth like exotic birds, only to be trodden to pulp under the endless shuffle and tramp of feet.

There was a small row of dingy shops by the bus stop: a newsagent, a greengrocer and an off-licence that sold cheap beer and spirits. Through the window of the off-licence I could see the owner, a small Indian man with a bald head, sitting safely behind a thick metal grille, which separated him and the cash register from troublesome customers.

'Is this really necessary?' I asked one day out of curiosity.

'Oh yes,' he replied in a polite and gentle voice. 'You know how it is, the local lads like to play tough, get themselves a bit of easy money.' He reached out and touched the grille fondly. 'This makes it simple. No problem for me. No problem for them.'

How awful to spend your life living in a cage, I thought to myself as I walked out. But then I remembered that most of us are living in cages of one kind or another and at least his was easy to see. Unlike my own. For instead of a metal grille, my cage was invisible and multi-faceted, like a finely cut diamond, and rather than being behind bars I was held captive by my own thoughts, fears, expectations and negative beliefs. Things that had become so habitual and ingrained that I had become unconscious of them.

Since my trip to Oregon I was increasingly aware of the degree to which I was imprisoned by my conditioning as a whole. But I was frustrated to discover that knowing this was not in itself the key to freedom. Actual freedom could only be won patiently and painstakingly by making my conditioning conscious one piece at a time, because it was only when I could see each individual thought or fear that I could begin to release myself from it.

One Saturday afternoon, I was browsing through a department store in a local shopping centre, when I was suddenly enveloped by an unmistakable smell. The smell of lilies. The smell of my mother. I looked around me with a wild surge of hope. Surely it had all been a dreadful mistake and here she was at last! The smell had come from the other side of the shelf and before I even had time to think, I dashed around, expecting to find Tate standing in the next aisle. Instead there was a young woman with a bottle of Diorissimo, Tate's favourite perfume, in her hand. I stood there for a moment gaping like a madwoman. Then it hit me. It had been over two years since Tate had died and yet I felt a wave of disappointment and shock go through me, as fresh and powerful as if I were learning of her death for the first time. My legs buckled underneath me and I lurched out of the shop, heart pounding, mind reeling.

I staggered on to the bus back to my university hall of residence and sank down in a seat by a window. I was trembling all over and I wrapped my arms tightly around my body, as if to prevent myself from falling to pieces. It was frightening to realize that the trauma of her death was still so present in my body. The grief and devastation of it all hadn't miraculously gone away, and sitting there on the bus I understood for the first time how seriously hurt I was. Separated from my day-to-day consciousness by a thin, frozen layer of denial lay a wound so big I had no idea what to do with it, except go on pretending that it wasn't there.

Tentatively, like a forensic scientist surveying a bomb-site, I began to assess the extent of the damage. I eased my way gingerly around the edges, measuring the space that this wound occupied inside me. It was immense. Far bigger than the actual size of my physical body and yet somehow it was contained within me. I knew it must hurt. But it didn't. I was still too numb to feel anything more than a dull, throbbing ache and a yearning, a constant yearning for what had been lost, as if part of me had been amputated.

How, I wondered, am I meant to live with this? Is this

it? Do I just keep pretending to be fine, while all along I have got this aching, gaping, living wound inside me? Surely, I thought, as a familiar question returned to me – a question that has truly been my saving grace – life doesn't have to be like this? Does it? I didn't know anybody who could answer that question. I knew plenty of people who were in pain, because I could see it clearly written across their faces. But no one I knew had figured out how to heal it. Endure it, yes. Transform it? Was that even possible?

There was a young man in my year called David. His life had also been turned upside down by tragedy when his mother committed suicide the year before. Like me, he had simply shut down in order to survive, taking shelter from his grief and pain, as if these emotions were a tidal wave that would sweep through and destroy him. One afternoon we were sitting together in the coffee bar, on either side of a stained Formica table, on squashy orange vinyl benches, surrounded by the usual crowd of raucous students. It was hardly the environment for personal revelation and yet David began to talk a little about what happened after his mother died.

'After the immediate feelings of shock,' he said, 'I went numb. Everything went grey and empty. I couldn't see the point of doing anything. Even being here –' he glanced round the coffee bar '– I'm only here because I have got to be somewhere, not because it means anything.' As I listened to him I saw how his unfelt pain and grief was colouring his entire life. It is like wearing the proverbial rose-tinted glasses, I thought, except the picture isn't very rosy.

David talked on, but I was only half listening, for my

mind was racing. This is what happens, I realized, putting the pieces together. Our lives get taken hostage by our past, because we carry within us everything that is unhealed – the pain, grief, loss, fear, anger – and instead of being temporary feelings these get stuck and become a permanent way of being. David is trapped in one particular event and his despair is so real to him that it's preventing him from seeing life as it really is – with all its potential for joy as well as sorrow. It's another form of mental prison and he doesn't know he's in it.

In a flash I saw myself in him and realized that of course I was trapped in just the same way. Everything I did and said was filtered through the lens of my mother's death. I glanced around at my fellow students. Despite their apparent gaiety and carelessness, I could see the traces of pain and suffering in many faces. We are all walking wounded, I thought, and I felt suddenly indignant. It is bad enough to have to go through the initial hurt or trauma, but then to be crippled by it for years, perhaps for an entire lifetime: that is the real tragedy. Surely, I thought again, life doesn't have to be like this?

Maybe, the idea came to me, answering my own question, these experiences stay in front of us until we learn how to heal. Except that we don't see them. We learn to look through them and push them away, ignoring how they are affecting our lives, because we don't know what else to do . . .

'Er, hello,' David said. 'I was talking to you . . .'

'Yes, I know,' I replied. 'I'm sorry, I was having a bit of a brainstorm. I was listening and I understand how unhappy you are. We both are. But you know what? I am sure it doesn't have to be like this. We can't help what has happened to us, but we can choose how it affects us. Right now we are imprisoned by the past, because we don't know how to deal with it. But there must be a way to heal the pain and despair. A way to get free. I don't know what it is or how to do it – but I am determined to find out.'

'Yeah,' he said doubtfully, draining his coffee cup and standing up, 'well be sure and let me know.'

As I walked across the college lawn to my next class, my mind was still racing. Maybe there is a gift in these wounds, I thought, because by learning how to transform the pain we grow stronger and wiser and more under-standing. Just like the heroes and heroines of myths and fairy tales – although the trials and difficulties they meet seem like disasters, they are actually essential to their growth and the resolution of their quest.

I felt my heart lift and surge with hope and optimism – for me, for David, for anyone who was trapped and hurting. I still didn't know how to heal, but that didn't matter, because I felt sure it was possible and I knew I could find out. I strode across the lawn, and like the hero-ine of any good fairy story I ran straight into my next obstacle. For I had gone no more than a few steps when another thought arose. David was different, a grim inner voice reminded me. He deserved to heal because he was innocent and I was not.

The image of Tate lying in a plastic bag flashed up in front of me, and as it had done hundreds of times before the accident replayed in my mind's eye. The sag in the bag as they carried her across the road. The light in my eyes so shockingly bright. The weight of her body press-ing on mine. My hands flying up off the steering wheel.

Hands now stained, like those of Lady Macbeth, with a blood I believed would never wash off. I felt suddenly ashamed. How could I have forgotten? My hope and determination drained away. That particular prison door, which had opened so unexpectedly, clanged shut and the padlock of my guilt clicked back into place.

5. Soul Stirrings

Every few weeks I went home from university for the weekend. It was hard to resist the pull of it. I missed Dad and Geoff and the dogs and cats. Missed the feeling of the house and the kitchen and my favourite spot by the Aga. And I missed the greenness and beauty – the garden and fields, the wide, open sky and the way the last, lingering light of sunset ebbed quietly into darkness.

The dirt and grime of New Cross, the constant thundering of traffic and the people with their pinched faces and blank eyes, distressed and depressed me. You're just a rich kid from the country who can't cope with the reality of the world, I told myself scornfully. But it wasn't that. Or at least it wasn't just that. Something essential was missing, buried beneath the dirt and concrete.

Back home that essential something seemed obvious – it was the connection to the sacredness of life. And as I walked over the downs, breathing in the sea-blown air and noticing the beauty all around me, my whole being expanded as I was touched again by the wild, unbounded joy I had experienced in Oregon. Surely, I thought, with a sudden clarity and certainty, this is what really matters, this feeling of awe and reverence for life, for its preciousness and its mystery.

Like the occasional flashes of intuition I had, this knowing seemed to come from a place deep within me. It was very different from my ego, the everyday 'me' I thought

I was, and yet it was more truly me than anything else. And each time I experienced it, I would suddenly feel nineteen years old going on ninety, or nine thousand, or ninety thousand, for there was no age and no limit to the awareness I felt inside. Where does that knowing come from? I wondered. Instinctively I felt it came from my soul, but what was that?

That question I couldn't answer, and yet there it was, a feeling of soul slowly starting to emerge within me, bringing with it this deeper level of inner knowing. At this point I just accepted that this knowing came in flashes of intuition and insight. Later on I would discover it is possible to access it all the time, for the still, small voice of the soul is always there, guiding us back home to the truth. It is just a matter of learning how to listen and to trust the guidance we are given moment to moment. And that would prove to be one of my greatest challenges.

But at the time it was surprising that I was thinking about my soul at all, because I was still vehemently and adamantly an atheist, just like my father. He remained utterly sceptical, not just of religion, but of anything remotely spiritual or metaphysical. 'Don't be so ridiculous, Bebe,' he scoffed when I told him I felt I had a soul. 'It's nothing more than biochemistry. What you fancifully think of as soul is simply an accidental function of the brain. It's all an accident. The fact that life exists at all is completely random.'

The rational and sceptical part of me agreed with him and I was alarmed to find myself straying into such intellectually dubious territory. Yet I couldn't help feeling there was more to life than mere mechanics. Much more. Something exquisitely precious, like a hidden jewel, shimmering at the heart of things. But whatever it was, this shimmering jewel, at least I was certain of one thing: it had absolutely nothing to do with God. To use the word soul was bad enough. To bring God into it was unthinkable. So the hidden jewel went without name or it went under other names like life-force or beauty or mystery. And I went on ignoring the split between what I felt inside and what I thought I believed.

So much at home was the same and yet so much was different, because my father had got remarried to an American woman called Vicki. They met in the summer of 1983, a year after Tate died. I first saw her at a party. It was a warm summer evening and all the guests were gathered outside on the terrace. Dusk was falling, wine was flowing, torches flamed around the garden. I had just got back from Oregon and I was sitting on a wall telling some friends about my trip, when I looked up and saw Dad talking to a beautiful woman I had never seen before.

She was wearing a white strapless dress and her glossy blonde hair was twisted up into an elegant chignon. I guessed she was in her late thirties. It turned out she was thirty-seven. My father was fifty-seven. I watched them together for a long, long moment. 'There she is.' The words flickered through my mind, not spoken, but heard just as clearly. 'Like it or not, she is the one.' I knew then that they would get married.

The ceremony was in September of the following year, just before I started university. After my initial shock when Dad told me, I felt pleased for him. I genuinely wanted him to be happy and I knew it was inevitable that he would remarry sometime. But on the eve of their wedding my deeper feelings hit me. How could he marry so soon? It was only two years since the accident and it still felt to me as if Tate was barely dead. This was her house. We were her children. Dad was her husband. Didn't any of that mean anything?

From their frozen smiles it was clear that Bon and Geoff felt the same way and I was terrified the moment had finally come when they would turn around and blame me. The words were so easy to say. I knew for I had already said them to myself a hundred thousand times: 'If you hadn't killed Tate, none of this would be happening.'

The marriage took place early on Saturday morning in a registry office and then we all came home for a blessing in the garden, arranged by Vicki. This was given by our local vicar, who found the whole thing 'most unusual'.

'She's American, isn't she?' he asked me conspiratorially.

'Yes,' I replied, 'from California.'

'Ah,' he said, 'that explains it.'

We stood together on the lawn and as the vicar droned on, the entire collection of family-owned dogs hurtled round the garden completely out of control. The whole thing seemed so surreal I didn't know whether to laugh or cry, but when Hercules, our large and unruly yellow Labrador, appeared from under the vicar's cassock doing the front crawl, Bon and I collapsed with laughter. Dad glared at us over his shoulder, the vicar read his final words, we all said 'Amen' and then we trooped back up to the house for a wedding brunch.

'Oh good,' said the vicar, grabbing a glass from a tray and gulping it with relief, 'champagne.'

Getting to know Vicki was a peculiar process. Here she was right in the very heart of my family and yet she was a stranger to me. I couldn't get to know her gradually, working my way in from a distance, building trust and intimacy as we got closer, because there was no distance. Not only that, I had no choice in the matter. I couldn't say, 'Actually, I don't like this one, could we please have someone else?' It must have been the same for her. She could redecorate the house, order a new bed and dinner service, but she couldn't tell Dad, 'Your children are awful, let's buy some different ones.'

With no choice my only option was to get on with her as best I could and I made a sincere effort to do so. In fact there was a lot to like about her. She was warm and welcoming and I never got the impression she would have preferred it if I stayed away. In fact she seemed genuinely interested in me, asking questions about university and my life in London. I would have happily confided in her, except for my lingering suspicion that she was just trying to win me over. Did she really like me or was she being friendly simply because it made her life easier?

Much more difficult was the thought that it was disloyal of me to like her. Am I betraying Tate, I wondered, if I am nice to Vicki? It seemed unfair to punish Vicki for something that was not her fault. Tate was dead. And Dad was right to go on living, to remarry and be happy. Yet I couldn't help but resent Vicki, for Tate's absence was made even more obvious by Vicki's presence.

It was Tate's house to the very core. She had dug the garden, helped rebuild the walls, designed and decorated it. Everything in it belonged to her and held memories of her. Even the little things. Especially the little things. One day I watched Vicki pull out a pair of Tate's old cake tins from a kitchen drawer. I wanted to snatch them away from her and shout: 'How dare you use those tins? Don't you know they belong to my mother?' I wanted to go and scream at Dad: 'How could you do this? How could you bring another woman into this house?'

Serenely unaware, Vicki buttered the tins, poured the sponge mixture she had made into them and put them in the oven, and I sat there politely and quietly, saying nothing. What is the point? I thought. It was not really about cake tins, or any of Tate's things. It was about wanting her memory to be acknowledged and honoured. But that I absolutely could not say. Instead I walked away, hiding my tears, resentment smouldering. If only I had been able to talk honestly. If only I could have said, 'This is how I feel', but I didn't know how to do that. No one in my family did. Instead we played out that which was unspoken over the dinner table.

Dad had encouraged all of us to cultivate logical thinking and the ability to hold our own in a debate. These skills were honed during dinner, where we had heated discussions about art, literature, science and philosophy. But on top of this, all the things that we never talked about directly – the hurts, grievances and jealousies – were played out unconsciously, giving an extra charge to the conversation. Ideas moved quickly and it often seemed more like fighting with daggers than words. Sometimes it became downright gladiatorial – a battle to the death and woe betide anyone unskilled at debate or unpractised in the arts of irony or sarcasm, because they were the first to bite the dust.

Vicki was at a distinct disadvantage. She was always eager to join in the discussion but she didn't have the training we'd had, nor did she realize what was actually at stake. Geoff and I would ruthlessly dismantle her argument, appealing to Dad to support us, knowing that he would have to be drawn in, bound by the rules of his own game. Vicki often left the table in tears and Dad, looking like a man caught between a rock and a hard place, would follow upstairs, to comfort her as best he could. Geoff and I remained looking innocently at each other across the table. After all, we had done nothing wrong and if she didn't like the game, then she shouldn't play it. But inside I felt sad and sorry. I knew I was being disingenuous, acting out the resentment I didn't dare state openly.

So it dragged on for months. Christmas passed. Spring came. Then one evening after Vicki had fled, Dad remained at the table, his head between his hands. At last he looked at me. 'Please go and talk to her,' he said, imploringly.

'Why should I have to go and talk to her?' demanded an angry voice inside. 'Why am I always the one who has to make things better?'

'Because you can,' replied a second voice, the voice of my soul. 'Because this is what it takes if you want to live your life based on love. It means acting kindly and honestly, saying and doing what you know to be right and true.'

'Oh, bloody hell,' I said to Dad, 'all right, I'll go.'

I stomped up the stairs, my heart pounding, feeling a curious mixture of courage and indignation. Vicki was lying on her bed crying. 'Look,' I said, 'I'm sorry. Really. I don't want to hurt you. I want you and Dad to be happy, but at the same time it is hard adjusting to you being here.'

She sat up, wiped her eyes and reached out to hug me. 'I know,' she said. 'I know how much you miss your mum and I'm really sorry that she's gone. I'm not trying to replace her, but I do love your father very much and I hope that you and I can be friends.'

In that moment I saw how hard she was trying and my

heart opened to her. As it did I discovered that loving Vicki didn't mean I loved Tate any the less, because there was plenty of room in my heart for both of them. And this convinced me more than ever that love was a better principle to operate from than anger. It also showed me that it was actually possible to resolve things by talking about them, because as soon as Vicki acknowledged Tate much of my resentment dissipated. Not that all the problems between Vicki and me were immediately and magically solved, and it took me several more years to develop a really close relationship with her and completely accept her presence in our lives. But from that point on I realized she wasn't the enemy and that allowed me to appreciate her for who she was and all the things she brought into our lives.

Like lettuces. Vicki not only rejuvenated Dad, she also gave a new lease of life to the vegetable garden. She brought packets of seeds with her from America – golden yellow squash, shaped like miniature flying saucers; long green snap beans and at least a dozen different varieties of lettuce, some of which ranked highly on the list of most beautiful things I had ever seen. There was one in particular. Its leaves were an exquisite pale and delicate green – very similar to the tiny translucent caterpillars that crawled in amongst them. But that green, remarkable though it was, was not its greatest beauty. For when you pulled the lettuce apart, inside at the heart, the leaves were veined and tinged with rose pink. It was a marvel to me. A stroke of genius on the part of someone in the design department, which I liked to imagine must exist somewhere in the universe.

With these wondrous lettuces Vicki made salad. Tossed with feta cheese, toasted pine nuts and home-made vinaigrette, they ranked highly on the list of most delicious things I had ever eaten. We had them for lunch at the table in the kitchen or, as the days grew warmer, outside in the courtyard, shaded from the sun by a new pretty pink-and-white striped umbrella. Geoff was there and sometimes Bonnie, with her first baby Beatrice. Vicki was about to give birth too and in a couple of months we would be joined by a baby brother – Valentine. Dad and Vicki radiated happiness and I felt happy for them, even though it was bittersweet. Why hadn't Dad and Tate been like this? I wanted to know. Had they ever loved each other so?

Thankfully by then I had a love of my own to turn to, because Ben and I started dating in May. Despite the immediate attraction between us, it had taken months to get over our mutual shyness and at times I wondered if we would ever even have a conversation. Then one Saturday he arrived at Grove Hall, my university hall of residence.

'Hi,' he said, looking adorably nervous. 'I wondered if you might like to come for a walk with me?'

'Now?'

He nodded.

'OK, let's go.'

Grove Hall lay on the edge of Greenwich Park and we walked around it for hours, finally stopping under the dancing green boughs of a chestnut tree. It was ablaze with flowers, great spikes of blossom like creamy white candles.

'Have you ever looked really closely at one of these?' I asked, pulling a branch down. 'Or smelt one?'

'In France,' he said, 'in the markets, you can buy honey that comes just from the chestnut tree: it tastes exactly like this smells.'

I looked at him in amazement.

I was in love.

We talked about everything. About his family and mine. About Tate and the accident. I told him things I had never told anyone. But there were plenty of things I couldn't tell even him. Like the sound of shattering glass. Or the silence that followed it. Or the images that still haunted me.

'Do you think about her much?' he asked gently. We were sitting next to each other, our backs resting against the tree. My chest tightened and tears sprang up. I looked away from him, up into the lace of green leaves. The question was too painful. Too close to the wound I pretended not to have.

'Only several times a day,' I answered in a flat voice, signalling the end of that particular conversation.

It was almost dark by the time we got back. 'I wanted to ask you something,' Ben said. There were roses blooming in front of the houses next to Grove Hall and he reached over a fence and picked one for me. Pale pink, petal upon petal – I was swooning as I smelt it. 'Would you go out with me? Again, I mean. To see a film or something?'

'Yes,' I replied, knowing perfectly well what he was really asking me, 'I would love to.'

6. Cracking Open

Before I knew it a year had slipped by and it was the beginning of my third and final year at university. Ben and I were more deeply in love than ever. He was smart, funny and kind and I sought comfort and refuge in him. In the warmth of his smile. In the beautiful nowness of his body. In the love that he offered me unconditionally. But wonderful as it was, the love we shared was not and could not be the solution to my problems and about halfway through the winter term, when I was twenty-one years old, I hit a crisis point.

It started gradually enough, one thing leading to another, until everything began to shift inside me. I think of a ship at sea, with its cargo neatly stowed and tied down tightly with ropes and chains. One day a storm approaches and the cargo begins to slip and slide, creaking and shuddering as it works its way loose, until it is sliding around the deck so violently that it threatens to overturn the entire ship.

My storm was the prospect of taking the final exams at the end of the third year. I had spent very little of my time at university actually studying and the consequences of this started to sink in. My father had told me all along that he expected me to get a first. But the weight of his expectation paralysed me, because it brought me face to face with my fear that he would only love me if I did brilliantly. As a child this belief was so painful that I stopped trying in school altogether, because it was safer to do nothing and only suspect that I didn't deserve his love, than try, fail and prove once and for all that I wasn't worthy. Which of course only reinforced the problem. 'But Bebe,' he used to say with disappointment, every time he read one of my very mediocre school reports, 'this really isn't good enough. I can't understand why you don't do better.'

Now I knew that if I didn't start working I was going to throw away my degree and for the first time ever I found myself wanting to do well. But if I did study it meant running the risk of failing and proving myself unlovable, which literally felt like facing death it was so terrifying. Both prospects were unbearable and together the pressure they exerted cracked me open – unleashing everything else that I had held in place for so long.

It happened suddenly. One moment I was walking along, coping with life as best I could. The next I felt as if I had dropped through a trapdoor into a deep, dark well of despair. I started to cry and couldn't stop. I collapsed on to my bed, unable to move, unable to eat, unable to do anything. Everything was black around me. I didn't notice the passing of day into night, didn't hear the birds or the traffic. It was as if the ordinary world had ceased to exist and I lay instead on the ocean floor, rocked by currents of emotion that ebbed and flowed completely beyond my control.

I cried and cried and cried. Most of the time I didn't even know what I was crying about and that was extremely frightening. What is happening to me? I wondered. Am I finally going crazy? But I didn't feel mad, for even in the midst of it all, there were moments when I could hear my soul calling to me from far away, as if it lay on the other side of the darkness that enveloped me. 'Hold on,' it said. 'Trust what is happening. You will be OK.'

In my mind's eye, I saw a golden thread, shimmering in the darkness.

'Yes,' said my soul, 'hold on to that, it will guide you.'

When it swept over me the darkness and grief was so overwhelming that nothing remained but the pulse, pulse, pulse of pain, seemingly infinite. It was all I could do to keep breathing. Then at other times I was lifted up out of the darkness to a higher viewpoint where I could see things clearly. In one such moment it occurred to me that my pattern of not working had developed as a survival strategy. In my child's mind it was the best thing I could come up with to protect me from the fear that I was unlovable. But now instead of protecting me it was severely limiting me and preventing me from achieving my best.

Good grief, I thought, something that started innocently enough, as a way of coping with a particular situation, has become installed as an automatic response to life, happening without my even noticing. I knew I had stumbled across something really important, not just this specific example, but as a principle of how our lives can be so dramatically affected by our past. I had an ominous feeling as I wondered how many other things I was doing equally unconsciously. Oh well, I comforted myself, as difficult as this is, at least I have seen it and that enables me to choose what I want to do. And I want to study: I don't want to ruin my degree because of a survival strategy that is no longer serving me.

After a couple of weeks the storm began to pass. The waves of grief and despair grew shorter and less intense. I lay in bed battered but alive. Soon I could get up. Soon

I could go out, and I resumed my life as if nothing had happened. Ben and I didn't talk about it and when my friends and teachers asked where I'd been, I said I'd had flu, because I didn't know what to else to say. It was years before it occurred to me that I'd had an emotional break-down and many more still before I could see that it was part of a bigger process of healing and becoming whole.

The winter term ended and I went home for Christmas and then returned to college in January. As usual, instead of 'I love you', my father's parting words were 'Work hard!' (If only I had realized then that, for my father at least, those two phrases amounted to the same thing.) 'You know I expect you to get a first!'

'Yes, Dad, I know,' I replied.

It didn't occur to me that my father thought I was so brilliant I was bound to get a first. Nor did I think to put an end to the doubt once and for all and ask him: 'Dad, do you love me regardless of what degree I get?' Instead the cold fear of failure swept through me and my new-found determination to study shrivelled up inside me like a tender seedling struck by frost. So there I was back at college and back at square one. Finals were six months away. Everyone else was already revising madly, including Ben, but I was just as paralysed by fear as ever and I spent each day sitting at my desk looking forlornly out of the window.

Then a couple of weeks into the term I went to a party and I met a young man called Nick who was studying psychology at Cambridge. To our mutual relief we discovered that neither of us were interested in social chit-chat and we were soon deep in a conversation about the nature of the psyche. As we talked, he quoted a simple saying of Carl Jung: 'We are not our emotions.' The words reverberated in my mind, and suddenly I got it. Of course, I thought, I am not my emotions! They exist inside me and the impact they have is immensely powerful, but they are not truly me.

'So wait,' I said to Nick, 'let me get this straight. It is the difference between saying "I am sad" and "I feel sad". In the first statement I am completely identified with sadness and there is no difference between me and it. In the second I am saying I have a separate identity that happens to be feeling sad in this moment.'

'Precisely,' he said.

'So then, what matters is not so much what the emotion is, but the degree to which we are identified with it.'

'Exactly,' he said.

The next morning I sat at my desk looking once again out of my window, not forlorn this time, but amazed. I am not my emotions! That thought, so profoundly simple, gave me distance and perspective. It enabled me to step back from the ongoing drama of my life and start cultivating a witness – a part of me that could watch what was going on without being so caught up or identified with it. Using that new-found awareness I tuned into the fear. It was still there, as terrifying as ever, and yet I was not as paralysed by it. So I can feel afraid, I thought, but at the same time I do not have to let it control me. Which means I can choose to do whatever I want – fear or no fear.

I began working furiously. About a month in, as I was writing essay plans for my exam on medieval literature, I discovered that actually I loved studying. I loved all the different ways of analysing and understanding an individual book or a genre of writers, and the essay questions bloomed like roses in my imagination. Damn, I thought with a sudden pang of regret, I have wasted so much time – my whole life at school wasted because I didn't dare to try.

Yet even as I discovered the satisfaction of working, every time I turned a page the shadow of my fear flickered across it. It no longer paralysed me, but it hadn't gone away either. It was simply on hold, put to one side in the 'pending' tray. The underlying belief that I wasn't good enough was too big and ran too deep for me to fully grasp. All I could do at this point was decide how to act in relation to the fear it generated.

But that was enough. 'I am not my emotions,' I chanted to myself over and over again, like a spell to ward off evil, and went on working. At last it was over and I got my degree. Not the first my father wanted, but a 2:1, and that was good enough for me. The funny thing was that it was good enough for him too.

'Oh well done, Bebe,' he said, beaming. 'That's very good.'

I shook my head, as if I had water in my ears. 'What did you say?'

'I said well done, very good,' my father repeated.

'Oh, right, thank you, that's what I thought you said.' And I wandered off, thinking something is wrong with this picture – but I couldn't quite figure out what.

7. The Truth Will Set Us Free

When I left university in 1987 I was twenty-two years old. I knew I wanted to work in television making documentaries. I had watched them avidly while I was growing up. I loved learning about wildlife and the environment. About the arts and history and science and space. But most of all I loved learning about people's lives and their different points of view – whether they came from a village in Africa or a housing estate in Glasgow. These films gave me hope. I thought that if only people would make the effort to understand themselves and each other, many of our problems – violence, racism, hatred, war – could be solved, and I believed that television could help promote that understanding.

I got my first job working for an independent production company based in West Kensington. I was hired as a production assistant on a series about adult education, called *On Course*. It was hardly my dream come true in terms of saving the world, but it was a great programme to learn on, because it combined a live studio show with short pre-recorded video inserts, and I got to learn about every aspect of television from managing the budget to filming on location to writing the script for the studio.

It was incredibly creative and exciting and I strode around the office wearing a black polo-neck, a black mini-skirt, thick black tights and black loafers (this was the late 1980s after all, and black was the requisite media attire), thrilled by the challenge and the buzz of it all. But it was also extremely stressful. My fear of not being good enough had of course accompanied me from university, and although I appeared confident and capable, I was terrified that any day someone would discover the real me cowering inside and denounce me as a fraud and an impostor.

My personal anxiety was exacerbated by the fact that it was the nature of television to be immensely demanding and stressful. There were so many variables, from anxiety about finding a good story and participants, to the logistics of filming, to the frantic rush of editing and finally the incredible buzz of broadcasting a live show. On top of this was the incalculable pressure exerted by the potential of each programme – what it was possible to achieve in the imagination. There was always one more phone call that could have been made, or an extra shot that could have been filmed, or a better way of editing a sequence, and the real limiting factors like money, time and the need to eat and sleep were simply ignored in the desire to create the best film possible.

All in all, these factors made television a Mecca for perfectionists, myself included of course, although I didn't realize it at the time. So the whole building was full of highly creative, intensely driven, strung-out workaholics, all juggling with one near-disaster after another, and each day passed in a blur of activity, my nerves jangling and my stomach in knots, as I pushed myself to try harder and do better.

But no matter how busy I was on the outside, inside I felt the same nameless yearning and longing for happiness I had felt as a teenager. 'Is the restlessness that gnaws inside me simply part of who I am?' I wrote in my diary when

I was twenty-four. 'Is it part of being human to feel dissatisfied? In which case should I just ignore it or does it mean I am supposed to be doing something else with my life?' This longing was like an itch that never stopped and I wished it would go away, because I thought that without it I would be able to settle down and accept my life as it was.

Now I know how essential it was, for it was the longing for love and truth, the longing to discover my true self and return home to the source of my being. Although on a personality or ego level we forget who we truly are, deep down the soul remembers and is constantly trying to remind us. So if our soul is the inner spiritual compass that guides us back to the truth, then our longing is the rocket fuel that propels us through the journey. Which is why the loss of spiritual knowledge in modern life is so devastating, because we are taught to ignore our inner hunger or to try and do the impossible and satisfy it with material things like money and possessions.

Thankfully, I couldn't just ignore it and so I used the longing as a lodestar, comparing where I was with where I wanted to be. I began to think of myself as my own laboratory, trying to figure out from the wild and unruly experiment of life what worked and what didn't. What brought me closer to love, what brought fear? What brought happiness, what pain? What satisfied this longing that lived so powerfully in me?

With the aid of my newly discovered witness, I started to pay attention to what was happening in my daily life. It was a shock to discover how much of the time I was still acting on autopilot. My reactions and responses to situations; my prejudices, judgements and beliefs about things – in fact the way I behaved in any given moment – were so defined by my conditioning and who I thought I ought to be and what I thought I ought to do, that at times I wondered if any of it was truly me.

From that awareness I began asking myself the question: Who am I? I know I am not my emotions or my habits or the things I have come to believe about myself – embroiled in them all as I still am. I am not my parents and I am not my conditioning either. I am not even the person I appear to be. At least it's not the real me, or the whole me anyway. So, take all that away and who am I?

I am behaving like a robot, I thought, remembering the ominous feeling I'd had at university when I encountered my first survival strategy. This was disheartening and frustrating. Yet, I also felt quietly optimistic, because I knew that the way to find the real me and become free was to reverse the process and make conscious everything that had become unconscious. And I realized the only way to do that was to watch it all play out on the stage of life, while constantly questioning: Is this true? Where does it come from? What does it relate to in the past? And is it serving me?

As I paid attention it began to dawn on me that life is the most extraordinary mirror, for it reflects back to us, with flawless precision, exactly what is going on inside. Eventually I would understand that the external world is not just a convenient reflection of what is happening inside, but that it is actually created by what is happening inside. This is a difficult concept to grasp, because it is so radically different from the way we usually see life. We are accustomed to thinking that life happens independently of us and that we respond to it as best we can.

In other words, the external events happen first and our reaction comes second. But in fact it is the other way around.

In Buddhism, this is summed up by the saying, 'All we are is the result of what we have thought' – because it is our thoughts and beliefs that determine our experience of life and create the situations we find ourselves in. Therefore if we want to change what is happening externally – problems with relationships, challenges at work, things going wrong – we have to look within and change what we believe inside. And that is not an easy task, because it requires self-examination and an unflinching commitment to the truth, including the willingness to let go of our false beliefs and misunderstandings, no matter how much we are attached to them.

So it is hard work, but it is also extremely empowering, because instead of being the victims of circumstance – 'This is happening to me and it is out of my control' – it means we have the ability to create real change. It also means that life is showing us, in every experience, including the difficulties and setbacks we encounter, precisely where we need to heal and grow. Although at first I couldn't see the true order of cause and effect – inner first, outer second – initially it was enough just to see life as a reflection showing me what was happening inside, and equipped with this new awareness I went on paying attention as best I could.

I bought a two-bedroom flat in a scruffy, run-down and therefore affordable part of south London. Off the main road the streets were quiet and lined with sleepy little houses that had been divided in two. My flat was upstairs and it had a light and airy feel. At the back, steps led down to a ten-foot-square patch of bare earth that was advertised in glowing estate agent rhetoric as a garden.

My family were delighted. Glad – and relieved – to see me getting on so well with my life. Dad gave me a dining table and chairs, a set of plates and some old and favourite orange cast-iron Le Creuset saucepans. 'Your mother and I bought this table,' he said fondly, as we loaded it into the back of a U-Haul, 'when we first lived together.' He and Vicki waved goodbye from the driveway as I set off to Bonnie's house. She gave me flowery curtains, sheets and blankets and an assortment of mugs and glasses and kitchen utensils. 'Thank you, thank you,' I called to her out of the window as I drove off.

Ben and Frances, my best friend from the Isle of Wight, moved in with me. We set about redecorating, stripping the walls of their hideous green-and-brown fern-patterned wallpaper and the floor of its equally vile swirly orange carpet. Frances and I painted the walls and ourselves white, while Ben got busy with the drill and put up bookshelves. We made reconnaissance trips to the local garden centre and planned what to grow in such a tiny space. We invited friends over for dinner and on Sunday afternoons we lazed around and watched the *Antiques Roadshow* on TV.

As much as they could be, these were happy times, and yet the gap between my inner and outer world was greater than ever. From the outside I appeared to have everything. Years later, one of my friends said to me, 'I remember seeing you at a party, just after you had bought your flat, and thinking that you, more than anyone else I knew, seemed to have the perfect life. You were beautiful, funny, smart and incredibly charming. You had a great job and a fantastic figure, you wore amazing clothes, you had a wonderful boyfriend and you were always off doing wild and exciting things. You seemed so confident and self-assured, as if you didn't have a care in the world. In fact it was hard not to be jealous of you.'

'If only you had known how tortured I was on the inside,' I replied, 'you would have pitied me instead.'

Looking back I can see that what she said was true – I did have a great life, and so much to be thankful for. But now I also know that until we come to peace with ourselves and heal the pain we carry inside, we can never be truly happy or appreciate what we have, no matter how wonderful the outer circumstances of our life. And at that time, not only was I still plagued by self-doubt, I was also doing my best to go on ignoring the bomb-site in my chest. Still there. Still raw and festering. Still waiting for me to learn how to heal it, and therein lay one of its gifts. For every experience, no matter how difficult or painful, contains an opportunity to learn and grow. This is the alchemy of life, because we learn how to turn the lead of tragedy and suffering into the gold of compassion and wisdom. But in order to heal and harvest the gift in the wound, you have to know how, and I didn't. And because of the guilt I felt, I was also still convinced that I didn't deserve to.

Barely a day went by that I didn't think of Tate. I was reminded of her every time someone said the word 'mother'. Every time I saw a woman out shopping with her children. Every time I turned on the TV to a film or family drama. Every time. It had been seven years since the accident. She would have been sixty-three, and I tried to picture her getting older. Sometimes Bonnie and I talked about her. 'Do you wonder what she would be like now?' I asked.

'Yes, of course. But it's better this way,' she said consolingly. 'Really, she would have hated to get old.'

It didn't feel better to me. 'Guilty, guilty, guilty, guilty, guilty . . .' I no longer even heard the words, but they pulsed inside me as regular and insistent as the drumbeat of my heart. The guilt had simply become a part of me, accompanying me everywhere, and I had resigned myself to it, like someone who walks with a limp or lives in constant pain. Not *like* someone who lives in constant pain: I *was* living in constant pain. With the aid of my witness I watched all this play out too, but it seemed beyond questioning. 'I killed my mother,' I would remind myself harshly. 'Of course I feel guilty, of course it hurts. What else do I expect?'

I was still haunted by memories of the accident. I might be eating breakfast or in the middle of a film shoot when suddenly an image or a sensation would burst into my mind: letting go of the steering wheel, the sound of smashing steel, the weight of her body pressing down on mine. It was like living in my own personal earthquake zone. While my world rocked, the rest of life went on as normal. Ben and Frances would go on eating toast as if nothing had happened. The camera crew would turn to me and ask, 'OK – what next?' Ever competent and capable, I would brush the memories aside and get on with the job. 'Well, it's a wrap here,' I'd reply. 'Let's break for lunch, then drive to the next location.'

I loved life so passionately, and yet there were many times when I longed to be dead. When I wished again that I had died in the car instead of Tate. Keats' words echoed frequently through my mind: 'For many a time / I have been half in love with easeful Death . . . Now

84

more than ever seems it rich to die, / To cease upon the midnight with no pain.' Easeful death – it did seem like it would be so much easier. If only I could just disappear or melt away, I thought, then I wouldn't have to deal with any of this, and there were moments when I seriously reconsidered committing suicide. Yet the soul force in me, deeper and more powerful than my despair, was determined to live, was struggling desperately in fact to be born fully into this world.

So I didn't kill myself. Instead I went on working. One of my best friends in television was called Edmund. We worked together on *On Course* and when we met his father had just been diagnosed with cancer. Over the ensuing three years I often listened as he talked about his grief and anger, and the pain and difficulty of watching someone he loved die. In turn he was one of the few people at work I told about the accident with Tate.

'Oh my God,' he said, hugging me. 'You poor, poor thing. I cannot imagine how awful it must have been.'

The image of Tate lying by the side of the road flashed into my mind's eye.

'I can only imagine how awful it must be for you,' I said, quickly brushing his sympathy and my memories aside. 'But at least you can say goodbye. Say the things you need to say to feel at peace with him – no matter how hard that might seem. Don't let him die and still be wondering if he really loved you. Thank him for being your father and tell him you love him. It won't make the pain go away now, but it will mean it hurts less later. Trust me.'

After his father died, Edmund starting seeing a therapist in order to work through his feelings. I looked on with a mixture of admiration and jealousy, wondering what it would be like if I could do the same. I was painfully aware of how much effort and energy it took to keep my guilt and grief under control, and I often thought about going to therapy myself. But my guilt had always prevented me from doing so. 'Guilty, guilty, guilty . . .' the words hummed on inside me, but for the first time I began to question them.

Eight years after the accident, I wrote in my diary: 'I am sure it is possible to free oneself from guilt. The purpose of therapy should not be to find answers of the "Why did this happen?" variety, because there are none. It should be to find a way of releasing yourself from whatever has happened. To accept it and to stop wanting so desperately for it not to have happened. This allows you to bring the energy dedicated to coping with the trauma back to yourself, to fuel your imagination and self-esteem and by doing so give yourself the best possible chance in life.'

Intellectually I understood it. The question was, did I deserve it? The answer came quite unexpectedly.

Glancing through the newspaper one morning, I noticed there was a documentary on television that evening about fatal accidents. Frances and I watched it together, squashing ourselves on to the small sofa in the living room. Frances sat down quite calmly with her knitting, but I was a bundle of nerves and glad to have her gentle, steady presence beside me.

The film consisted of interviews with four people who had been involved in an accidental death. One man had been giving his paralysed wife a bath when the phone rang. He went to answer it and by the time he returned a few minutes later, his wife had slipped beneath the surface of the water and drowned. He said how he longed to be able to talk about it with someone who could really understand. How the guilt gnawed away at him every day.

'Have you considered ending your own life?' the interviewer asked.

'Yes,' he replied, 'I think about it every day.'

My heart ached as I listened to him. It was so much easier to feel the depth of his pain than it was to feel my own. And yet feeling his suffering brought me face to face with mine. I shifted about on the sofa in agony, not knowing whether to cry or run.

Hard as it had been listening to the first man, it was the testimony of a woman, a nurse, that most affected me. As she was driving home one day from the hospital where she worked, a child ran out from between a row of parked cars, right in front of her. It happened so quickly, she had no chance to brake or swerve and she hit the child, who died immediately. She was devastated by the accident. 'If only I could have stopped . . .' she lamented. 'If only I had driven another way . . . If only I had left work later . . . I will never be able to forgive myself . . .' The grief and misery she felt was etched across her face and her whole countenance was grey, as if she were the one that had died.

She expressed a deep belief in God, but instead of comforting her, it seemed to contribute to her misery. Despite her obvious anguish and sincerity, I felt no sympathy for her. In fact I felt angry. It was so clearly not her fault that it seemed ridiculous for her to torture herself with such unnecessary suffering. I also couldn't understand the gap in her faith and logic. If, as she claimed to believe, God was responsible for everything, then surely that included the giving and taking of life and therefore neither the accident nor the child's death were her fault at all.

The programme ended and Frances and I looked at each other. 'Oh Catherine,' she said, 'I couldn't imagine before what it must feel like for you. You never talk about it and I don't like to ask. Do you feel that desperate? Do you blame yourself in the same way?'

'Of course I do,' I replied. 'The accident was my fault. I killed her – my mother. There are no words to convey how awful that feels. They all talked about wanting forgiveness. But who do they want it from? The only person who could give it is dead.'

We went to bed and when I woke up the following morning I got on with life as usual. But over the next few days my mind kept going back to the nurse, painstakingly turning her story over and over, in a way that I have come to learn means there is something important that I have missed. I still felt angry with her. How stupid to go on blaming herself, I thought. As if what happened isn't bad enough anyway. And how arrogant to put yourself in the place of God! Suddenly I heard what I was saying. The words circled around and whispered themselves back into my own ear: how arrogant to put yourself in the place of God.

And I got it.

Deeply shaken, I saw that the nurse was a mirror for my own situation, because we were both blaming ourselves for something completely beyond our control. In that moment I realized I was not actually responsible for Tate's death. I had not meant to kill her and even if the accident was my fault, the outcome of it was not.

In that tiny, stony gap between cause and effect, forgiveness took root and flowered. The burden of guilt that I had carried for eight long years melted away. For days I was filled with euphoria. I wanted to dance, sing, leap, fly, dive, soar. I felt all the delight of a prisoner sentenced to death who is suddenly found innocent. It was not my fault, I chanted to myself over and over again, and each time it hit me with the amazing freshness of a revelation. Not my fault! Not my fault! I didn't kill her!

Each morning I woke up with the feeling that something was missing. Startled, I looked around me. Every-thing was the same. The battered iron-and-brass bed frame. The white walls and blue flowered curtains. The straggly trees outside in the garden and the row of red-tiled roofs of the next street, all quite plain and ordinary. So what was it? Then I'd remember. The guilt – it's gone: I didn't kill her. Relief would flood through my body and I'd sink back against my pillows and gaze out of the window, watching the pigeons strutting about on the roofs opposite, as I realized that all along the person I had needed forgiveness from was me.

8. Learning to Listen – Almost

It turns out that the truth really will set us free. For unless we are actually physically incarcerated, the prisons in which we live exist only as stories in our minds, in the lies we tell ourselves through our thoughts and beliefs, assumptions and expectations. Believing that I had killed Tate was just one of mine. There were dozens of others. Like the belief that I wasn't good enough or that it wasn't OK to be me. Then there are the collective stories that we live in. Such as the belief that money is the ultimate goal in life. Or the belief that the material world is all there is. In fact the majority of our conditioning – especially the things we most cling to – is based on stories and it is by seeing through them to the truth that we set ourselves free.

I didn't kill her! In the absence of my guilt I realized just what a prison it had been. Freed from it, the horizons of my world rolled wide open and as I danced and floated and dived and soared I felt again the feeling I'd had in Oregon of unlimited potential. It is my life, I thought, and I can do anything with it. I don't have to live out the rest of my days in expiation, trying to make amends for my crime. I cannot rewrite the past, but I can rewrite the future.

One morning, after about a week of euphoria, I woke up unusually early and as I was still half dreaming an image came to me. I had climbed out of a deep, dark hole and was standing on a large barren plateau. Everything was lifeless and grey. I looked in front of me and saw my future, blank and empty. I turned and looked behind me. There was my past, a chaotic jumble of emotional rubble and debris. I surveyed this inner landscape with shock and dismay.

Surely it can't be that bad? I thought. Secretly I had cherished the hope that if I could let go of the guilt then the rest of my life would be easy. I had also assumed that most of my unhappiness stemmed from the accident. With a horrible sinking feeling I realized that neither of those assumptions was true. It was just that my guilt had been so paralysing that everything else had been on hold.

Now that my guilt had gone – and that was still completely and utterly amazing – all the other things in me that needed attention and healing began to rise to the surface. Like my relationship with Tate, for instance. Again, I had hoped that if I could get over the accident then my feelings towards her would be simple. Now it struck me how very painful and difficult our relationship had been before she died, because of the uncertainty I felt about whether she loved me and my fear of being abandoned by her. My heart sank.

As I lay in bed looking at the pigeons still merrily strutting about on the roof opposite, as happy and unconcerned as they had been a few days before, a memory came to me of hiking in the mountains with my godmother, Joan. Sometimes as we climbed higher we came to a false summit. Thinking we were approaching the top, I would sink with disappointment as I staggered up it only to see the trail stretching on up the mountain before me. 'You just have to keep going,' Joan said one day, noticing I was some-what crestfallen. 'It's the only way to get there.'

I suppose this is the same thing, I thought. Important as it is, letting go of my guilt is not the end of the journey. In fact it is just the beginning of another stage. If I want to be happy and free, then I have no choice but to find a way to work through the rest of this emotional rubble. After all, I am carrying it inside me and it is affecting me whether I like it or not. So I have to take responsibility for it. My soul nodded vigorously and I felt a surge of resolution and determination. And, I thought, I can't do it on my own. I need help.

So once again I considered starting therapy. But there was no time to actually do anything about it, because I was about to finish one contract and start another. I had been offered a job as assistant producer on a popular series for BBC2, called *Rough Guide to Careers*. It was a big promotion and not only was I flattered to be chosen, I knew that it would look good on my CV. Even so I had serious reservations about taking it. I was always exhausted when I finished a job and normally I took a couple of weeks off to recover before starting another. In this case they ran back to back, which meant finishing on Friday and starting the new one on Monday. Should I take it? I wondered.

'No,' said my intuition.

'Of course you should,' said my ego. 'It's only another four months – we can take time off then.'

'Of course you should,' said everyone else. 'It's a great opportunity. You'd be mad not to accept.'

So I did. As assistant producer it was my job to research the content of the films and find all the interviewees, plus exciting and unusual locations to film them in. Which would normally have been fine, except on this particular series the schedule was very tight and we had half the regular research period. Within a week I was seriously worried about whether I could get everything ready in order to start filming on time, and I started working flat out.

I was already so tired I didn't have the resources to work that hard or to maintain a perspective about what was really happening. So instead of remembering that the schedule was virtually impossible, I started blaming myself, thinking that I was struggling because I wasn't good enough at my job. The fact that I had just been promoted created the ideal breeding ground for self-doubt, and my inner critic went crazy. 'If you were better, faster, cleverer, more talented, more capable . . . then you wouldn't be in this situation.' 'Look around you: no one else is having such a big problem. They are all managing just fine.' Which was true. The rest of the team were under a lot of stress, but no one seemed to be finding it as difficult as I was.

So I pushed myself harder and harder, until I felt like a wire that had been so tightly stretched it was quivering under the strain. I longed to simply stop and I began to count the days until the series would be over. If I can just make it to the end, I promised myself, I will take as much time off as I need to. But I didn't get that far. Halfway through the schedule I noticed a pale-pink rash on my stomach. The next day it had spread up across my chest. I went to my doctor, who said, 'Oh, don't worry, it's just a mild case of psoriasis. No one knows why these things happen. I'll give you some cortisone cream to rub on and that will take it away.'

The mild case of psoriasis had a mind of its own. As I went on frantically setting up interviews, my skin itched and prickled as if an army of ants were colonizing my body inch by inch. When I got home each night I cried at the prospect of taking off my clothes, because I dreaded seeing how much further it had spread. Within a few days it formed an ugly red sheet across my back. Within a week my entire body was covered with deep-red, scaly, itchy welts. With a certain irony, the only exceptions were my face and the backs of my hands, which meant that if I wore trousers and a long-sleeved shirt, I could maintain the appearance of being fine.

I went back to my doctor on Monday morning. She took one look at me, picked up the phone and referred me to the dermatologist at the local hospital. Luckily there was an appointment available in two days' time. From the doctor's surgery I went straight to see my series producer.

'I have to talk to you,' I said. 'I've got a rash.'

'Oh,' she said, slightly annoyed. 'Well, how bad can it be?'

'Er, really bad.' I hesitated, feeling very hideous and ashamed. 'Do you want to see?'

She nodded, so I slowly lifted up my shirt and turned around.

'Oh my God, Catherine,' she gasped, 'that is awful. What can I do? Do you want to leave?'

'I don't know,' I answered, on the edge of tears. I had never given up on anything and the thought of walking out on a job appalled me. 'I'm going to hospital on Wednesday, so let's see what the consultant says.' And I went back to my desk, picked up the phone and continued as if nothing were happening.

I arrived at the dermatologist's office and a young man sitting behind a desk looked up from some notes.

'So you have a sudden outbreak of psoriasis?'

I nodded, not trusting my voice to speak.

'OK, well let's take a look at you.' He pointed to a screen. 'Please take everything off except your underwear and put on the hospital gown.' I came back out and he looked at my back through the opening.

'How far does this go?' he asked.

'All over.'

'All over? Would you mind taking off the gown so I can see?'

I knew I would cry at any moment, so again I simply nodded and slipped the gown off.

'Oh dear,' he said, 'I've never seen anything like this.'

I could hardly bear it. He was supposed to be reassuring and tell me it would soon go away, not tell me that it was as truly awful as I thought it was. I dressed and sat down at the desk opposite him. He reached across the desk and handed me a box of tissues. 'The bad news is we don't understand the cause of psoriasis and we don't have a cure for it, but there are things that can help: cortisone cream, tar, radiation therapy.' He started to write out a prescription.

'Rest is also important. What work do you do?'

'Television – assistant producer.'

'So you are under a lot of stress?'

By this time I was weeping profusely into the tissues.

'That has to stop. You can blame it on me. I will write a letter recommending you leave. That way your employer can claim any expenses incurred against their insurance. Will you leave?'

I nodded and immediately a tremendous sense of relief surged through my body.

'Good. I want you to come for your first radiation treatment next Monday. Unless you can go and get some sun. Sunshine is the best remedy there is. Could you do that?'

The year before, my father and Vicki had bought a house in the south of France. They were staying there for the summer and had rung me just a few days earlier, urging me to come and visit. I imagined the brilliant blue skies, the warm, fragrant air of the afternoons and the sound of the cicadas pulsing in the heat. Something in me was rejoicing. I felt as if I had been plucked from hell and now I was going to heaven. Snapping out of my reverie and back into the hard hospital chair, I told the doctor I could go to Provence.

'That's perfect. Stay as long as you can,' he said, as he pushed a prescription towards me.

'How long will it be before it goes away?' I asked.

He stopped abruptly, hand still on the prescription. 'You had better prepare yourself,' he replied. 'Psoriasis doesn't often go away. Once it occurs it is generally a lifelong condition, especially when it's as serious as yours.'

My heart stopped beating for a moment.

'There is a support group, though,' he added, as if that was a consolation. 'I'll give you their number.'

That night when I got home, I went into my bedroom, took off my clothes, stood in front of the mirror and looked at myself carefully. My skin was truly shocking and I felt a tremendous sadness. Am I really going to be like this for the rest of my life? I wondered. Tenderly, I stroked my tummy and as I ran my fingers over the bumps and welts, it dawned on me that my body had simply externalized how I felt about myself inside. The poison of my self-doubt had finally leaked out, staining my skin with the unmistakable evidence of how harshly I was criticizing myself.

Suddenly, I saw myself as I had been two weeks before. I mean really saw myself. And saw how beautiful I was. I don't mean by model or Hollywood standards, I mean beautiful in the way that human beings are beautiful. Two legs. Two arms. Breasts. A tummy. Smooth skin. All working. All healthy. Amazing! Beautiful!

Then I saw myself again as I was now. Oh, my God, I thought, what have I been doing? I traced the curves of my arm and the fullness of my breasts. There is absolutely nothing wrong with me. Yet I am always judging myself for not being good enough, including my poor body – for like virtually every other woman I knew I constantly worried that I should be thinner.

Finally, standing there in front of the mirror, I saw my beauty and I saw the beauty in all of us and it had nothing to do with being fat or thin. But it took until my skin erupted into hideous red scales for me to really get it. It is all madness, I thought. The obsession with weight is just another way to judge and hate myself. I am never enough. Not thin enough, not beautiful enough, not smart enough . . . And now look at me. See what all that hatred has come to. 'Oh my poor, poor body,' I said softly, lovingly. 'If you heal this, I promise I will never criticize you again. I will be deeply grateful for and appreciative of my true beauty and I will learn to stop hating myself, whatever that takes.'

Dad, Vicki and Valentine, now five years old and an adorable blond-haired little boy, met me off the plane. Vicki's eyes scanned me anxiously as we waited to collect my bag.

'It's all covered up,' I explained, acknowledging her unspoken question, 'but I'll show you later if you want.'

She nodded.

'Well,' said Dad, in his making-the-best-of-things voice, 'whatever the reason that brings you here, we are delighted to have you.'

My father had always wanted to live in France. When I was a child we used to go there every year, mostly to Brittany, on a combined business trip and family holiday. My father owned an oyster fishery and although it seemed rather like taking coals to Newcastle, he sold a lot of his stock to French shellfish suppliers.

Most of the holiday time was spent on the beach, exploring the rock pools left naked by the retreating sea, with their huge, bright-orange starfish, vivid against the slick, dark rocks, and strange sci-fi spider-leg crabs that scuttled through the tangled seaweed. But when we were not thus occupied we drove around the countryside look-ing for ruined houses and barns. When we spotted some-thing suitably derelict we would pile out of the car, fight our way past brambles and overgrown bushes, step through the mouldering doorway and into a crumbling framework upon which my father could hang his dreams.

It had remained a dream until one day the previous summer I received an excited call from Dad. 'Guess what?'

'What?'

'We've bought a house.'

He and Vicki were visiting Provence and instead of the building site Dad longed for, they had found a very simple farmhouse, perched on the edge of a hilltop village, look-ing out over a valley of vineyards and across to some thick forested hills.

As we drove through the countryside I was amazed to see the paintings I had studied in art history brought to life. It was classic, rural Provence, unchanged since Van Gogh wandered through the hills, painting not just the product of a frenzied imagination, but literally what he saw. Golden fields of wheat, molten in the searing midday heat. The gnarled and twisted shapes of the cypress trees, swaying and dancing with their own inner life-force. The sun, a blazing ball in the sky, beating down on the olive trees, bent and dusty like the backs of the old men who tended them.

The house itself was cool and comfortable and it was bliss to be there. Bliss to wake up and remember that I was free from the nightmare of schedules and deadlines. Bliss to wander outside and find Dad and Vicki lingering over breakfast. Bliss to have day after day with nothing planned. I spent many afternoons lying in a hammock under the shade of the mulberry trees, drifting with the sound of the cicadas, a book – pages unturned – open on my chest. In the evenings we had dinner outside and watched as the sky flamed orange and red, before darkening through violet and purple into a blue so deep and dark you could swim in it to infinity.

On Saturday mornings Vicki and I went to the market in the nearby medieval hill town. It took place in the main square and overflowed into the network of narrow cobbled streets that fanned out from the centre. As well as fruit and vegetables, there were stalls of every kind. One of my favourites sold hand-milled soap, perfumed with lavender and rose and lemon and enriched with local olive oil. Next door there was a bright array of multi-coloured wicker baskets. Vicki and I bought one each to carry our many purchases.

The stalls were in the same place each week and we soon came to remember where we had found the best olives and the ripest tomatoes. Yet there was still the pleasure of the unexpected. An old peasant farmer, for instance, face brown and wizened, who had cycled into town, balancing a shallow basket containing a dozen little pats of handmade goat's cheese, snowy white against a lining of glossy green leaves. So we took our time, stopping to examine each stall, sampling the produce and chatting to the vendors in my truly terrible French.

Then we set about the serious business of shopping. Every week we bought more or less the same things: fresh crusty bread, tomatoes, olives, goat's cheese, salami, mixed salad leaves, onions, garlic and mussels – which would make *moules marinière* for lunch that day – and fabulous white-fleshed peaches and nectarines, so ripe and fragrant they perfumed the car on the way home.

I know it is naive to think that a place one visits on holiday is somehow exempt from ordinary struggles and difficulties, but I was struck by the pace of life there. The local people were connected to the land, to the rhythms of each day and the passing of the seasons. The emphasis was on simple tastes and pleasures and, as Oregon had done years before, it reminded me that there *was* a different way to live. And on reflection I couldn't say whether my life in London with its hectic sense of achievement and importance was any better than this one, so slow and appreciative, that I saw being lived all around me.

Within a few weeks my skin started to become clear and so did I. With time to sleep, relax and reflect, my sanity slowly returned. Maybe it really was the schedule that made things so difficult, I thought. Therefore I was criticizing and doubting myself for nothing. Why do I do that? Why do I automatically assume it is my fault? Or that I am not good enough?

'I realize how important it is to me not to be thought stupid,' I wrote in my diary. 'One, because I have this sense of perfection that I need to achieve. Secondly, because I still have a huge lack of confidence in my intelligence and I am terrified that I will soon be found out, exposed and revealed as stupid. And that when I am found out, people won't like me any more. So it is not just a lack of confidence in my intelligence, it is a deep lack of confidence in myself overall. It comes from the past, from a time when I did not feel valued or appreciated for who I am. Now I am being controlled by the belief that I am not good enough, and that is simply not true.'

To my dismay, unlike the belief that I had killed Tate, the belief that I was not good enough didn't immediately dissolve upon contact with the truth. Some things are so deeply ingrained that they do not just go away. Instead it is a matter of learning to work with them and gradually release the stranglehold they have upon us. First we have to notice what our beliefs and behaviour patterns are. Then we have to question if they are true or helpful. If they aren't then we have to actively choose to believe what *is* true and to behave in a new and positive way. So seeing the truth revealed my belief to me. It unmasked it as a story and a habit of mind, no matter how deeply ingrained. From there it was a matter of learning to recognize when I was beating myself up for not being good enough, and to remind myself – over and over again – that it was not true, and tell myself instead that I am perfectly OK as I am.

So I was starting to learn about myself – to see the major patterns and fault lines of my personality – and about the process of healing and transformation itself. I was also learning about the connection between my mind and body. The fact that the psoriasis cleared up so easily convinced me that my body had created it as a result of all the criticism I had heaped upon myself and also because I had pushed my body too far. If only I had listened to my intuition, I thought, and turned down the job on *Rough Guides*, I probably wouldn't have ever got psoriasis. The trouble was I wasn't used to listening to my intuition, not when it came to making decisions like that anyway, because like so many people I had learnt to rely on my rational mind and ego instead. So I did what seemed logical or sensible or what I thought I 'ought' to do. Now I started to wonder if that approach was quite as reliable as I thought.

After six weeks, I went home. Back in my flat, I lay on the sofa, wondering what to do next. Although I was feeling much better, I knew I wasn't physically ready to go back to work. My body groaned at the very thought of it, and my intuition whispered silently to me that I needed adventure, something to nourish the wild, free-spirited part of me. This time I was willing to listen and I remembered Joan telling me about a white-water rafting trip she had taken on the Colorado River, through the Grand Canyon. 'Yes, yes!' my intuition said. I rang the rafting company, and it turned out that their last trip of the year started in just a few weeks, with the option to go for seven, eleven or twenty-one days. My spirit soared at the prospect of spending three weeks on the river, but it cost over $2,000 . . .

I rang Joan. 'It seems awfully expensive,' I said doubtfully.

'You won't regret a single penny,' she said. 'It's one of the most wonderful trips I have ever taken and I know you will love it. Do you have the money?'

'Well, kind of . . .'

'Then spend it.'

It was true, because I had worked solidly during the last year, I did have the money. But there was always the uncertainty of not knowing when I would have another job, and that made me hesitate to spend so much on a holiday. On the other hand, I remembered that we all live with the constant uncertainty of not knowing anything. For if Tate's death had taught me one thing, it was that life could end at any moment. Who knows, I thought, I could be run over by a bus in six months' time and then it won't matter how much money I have.

Knowing this wasn't depressing or frightening. Accepting my own mortality was immensely liberating and life-enhancing: instead of fearing or denying death I welcomed it as my ally. It gave me permission to live my life in a different way – instead of focusing on what I ought to do or what would be safe, I found myself asking: How can I live life most fully? It was motivating too. Now is the only moment I have got, I told myself, and I rang the rafting company back and said, 'OK, I'll do it: twenty-one days.'

9. Feeling the Flow

My first sight of the Grand Canyon was from the air. To say that it was breathtaking would be an understatement. It was more like feeling a shock wave of awe pass through my body. I was staggered by the beauty of it. By the immensity. The complexity. The exquisite colour and shading of the rocks. The 'now you see it, now you don't' glistening jade green of the Colorado River, winding between the canyon walls.

I met up with the rafting company and the rest of the group at a motel in Flagstaff. As we introduced ourselves I looked around curiously at my fellow adventurers. Out of twenty-five people there were only two other women: Paula, a lawyer, about ten years older than me, and Jan, the trip cook, who was my age. The oldest person, an elegant, silver-haired Frenchman called Roger, was seventy. It was hard to imagine him plunging through freezing cold, life-threatening rapids. But when it came to his turn to introduce himself he said he had rafted and kayaked down every major river in the world and that this was his third and final trip on the Colorado. 'After this I will retire,' he said. 'Alas, white water has been my greatest passion, but I am getting too old, my life is coming to a close.'

'Not many people have died on this river,' said Bronco, the head guide, as he began his briefing. 'But it is possible. The rapids are dangerous. You can get thrown out of the boat. Once in the river the water is freezing. Cold enough to kill you, if you don't get smashed to pieces on the rocks first.' He paused to see if his words were having an effect. 'While we will do our best to make sure you are safe, you also have to do your part. You have to obey instructions and you have to hold on tight. We will go through the safety procedures tomorrow when we get to the boats. Meanwhile, your task for this evening is to learn how to pack your gear into one of these waterproof bags.' He held up a heavy rubber bag. 'But that's tiny,' whispered Paula, who was sitting next to me. 'I'll never get all of my stuff into that.'

The following morning we drove to the start of the Canyon, at Lees Ferry, just below Glen Canyon Dam. The boats – finely crafted wooden dories – were already there, rocking invitingly on the swirling current. The river was broad and calm, flowing between cream-coloured limestone cliffs, which soared up above us. Just downstream the Canyon turned to the left and the river disappeared around the bend, mysterious and tantalizing.

The guides fitted us with life jackets, showed us how to stow our carefully packed gear and gave us a safety briefing. After completing what seemed like an interminable list of last-minute details, we were ready to set off. Each boat held three or four people, plus a guide to row it. 'Get in any boat you like,' Bronco said. 'We'll swap around every day, so you'll have the chance to travel with everyone.'

I found myself sitting in the front of a boat next to a man in his mid-fifties called Keith. Paula and a doctor in his early thirties called Sean sat in the back. 'Feeling brave, are you?' asked Dougald, our guide for the day, looking at Keith and me. He had a serious face, with features chiselled in the mould of a Roman emperor's, but his dark-brown eyes were lively and mischievous.

Keith and I looked at him blankly.

'The front of the boat,' he said. 'It's where you get the biggest ride and the wettest and we'll be going through some mighty big rapids today, yes sirree.' And he whistled quietly to himself as he prepared to push off from shore. 'Seriously, folks,' he added, looking around at all of us, 'we're going through some rough white water today, so when I tell you to hang on, you hang on tight, OK?'

With that he pushed off. The boat slid out across the slick water, spun for a moment as she righted herself in the current and then we were swept away. Day after day this was my favourite moment. The moment when we gave ourselves to the flow of the river. Each time I felt it deep in my body, in my bones – a 'yes', a rejoicing surrender to the flow of life, the deep undercurrent that is always there, always ready to carry us home.

As soon as we left the bank, Sean began grilling Paula about who she was and what she did. Soon he wanted to know about Dougald and then Keith and me. When it was my turn I kept my answers short. I had already decided to give most of my attention to being in the Canyon itself. I didn't want the trip to end only to find out that I had missed the whole thing because I was too busy talking and trying to charm and please. 'I didn't come here to be sociable,' I wrote in my diary. 'This is my time and I don't care what people think of me, even if they think I am rude or boring or selfish – the cardinal sin.'

So I listened to their chit-chat with one ear. With the other I started tuning into the greater conversation of water and wind and rock and sky that was happening all around us. The rippling of the river as it rolled over the stones. The golden leaves of a cottonwood tree shivering in the breeze. The whir of wings as ducks startled up from the shore. The exquisite cascading song of a canyon wren echoing across the water. Beneath it all was the silence – a living presence, out of which all other phenomena arose.

Our days had a certain rhythm and symmetry to them. We rose as the first rays of sun kindled fire across the upper canyon walls and packed our tents and gear while Jan made breakfast. At sunset we pulled ashore and reversed the process, making camp while Jan cooked. After dinner we sat round the fire, tired and content, sharing stories and singing songs. In between we surrendered to all the unknowns that each day would bring – a visit to some Anasazi ruins, the unexpected grace of a heron in flight or a sudden drenching from an afternoon rainstorm.

Of course there were the rapids too, which punctuated our day like the timpani drums punctuate a symphony. Exhilarating as they were, I loved the stillness that followed more. Swept along by the river, through one winding canyon after another, I found myself utterly enthralled. 'I keep being drawn into the age of the place,' I wrote. 'Every moment is like sinking back in time. I am steeping my soul in eternity. An eternity I am part of – not separate from. It is not an other-worldly heaven, but an eternal cycle of life and death. I embrace the cycle. I love the idea of being alive, here and now, and of one day melting back into the earth, releasing my spirit, my energy, to reunite with the indefinable substance that surrounds us.'

As the days slipped by the distractions, pressures and

worries of the outside world began to lose their importance. After the first couple of days it no longer mattered
that I didn't have a hairdryer or a mirror. After a week I
stopped missing the newspaper, the TV and the telephone.
In the space and silence my mind cleared and quietened.
'The river develops or has the potential to develop a new
emotional awareness,' I wrote. 'As a process it is like
panning for gold: the river washes away the sediments,
tiny stones, mud, shale, all the debris, leaving the larger
sections of emotion – both good and bad – exposed like
nuggets of gold.'

The rafting company had supplied a couple of inflatable two-man kayaks for us to use on the quieter sections
of the river and – if we dared – through some of the
smaller rapids. Sean and I soon became kayaking buddies,
because he was the only one willing to brave the rapids
with me. One morning after we had paddled for dear life
through a thundering blur of water and stone, the river
turned around a bend and entered into a beautiful stretch
of canyon. Pale sandstone walls soared up hundreds of
feet above us, while the river flowed on thick and slow
and utterly serene.

We put down our paddles and stretched out in the
kayak, feet dangling luxuriously over the edge. As we
drifted with the current, Sean resumed his ongoing inter-
rogation about my life. Americans, I had noticed, were so
much more direct in asking questions than English people,
and Sean was more direct than most.

'So how did your mother die?' he wanted to know.

'In a car accident.'

'Were you in the car with her?'

I couldn't believe he had actually asked me.

'Yes.'

'How old were you?'

'Seventeen.' In the silence that followed I held my breath and waited. Would he ask me the next, the obvious question?

'So, who was driving?'

'Do you know that in eight years you're the only person who has ever asked me that?'

'So, who . . . ?'

'I was.'

As I answered him, once again the whole thing replayed in my mind's eye as vivid and visceral as the day it happened. A wave of nausea swept through me as I sat there in the kayak, my body trembling and my heart pounding.

'What's happening?' Sean asked. 'You've gone very pale.'

'Oh, nothing,' I replied, struggling to regain my composure. I looked up and saw the rest of the boats disappearing around the next bend. 'We'd better get paddling.'

That night, I left the fireside early. I crawled into my sleeping bag and got out my torch and my diary. 'The memories are as powerful as ever,' I wrote. 'I guess it is evidence that the accident is still held inside me, a wound unhealed and in need of healing. I want to be free from this pain. After my dream about Tate the other day, I know she would want me to be free from it also.'

Just before starting the trip I had dreamt about Tate – a very rare occurrence. She and I were standing in a kitchen. There were quite a few other people around, but I don't remember who they were. Tate was at the stove cooking bacon and getting irritated by the fact that people were milling about and not saying whether they were hungry. I was standing next to her, feeling anxious because

I could see she was getting angry and I didn't want her to be angry with me.

She turned to me and said, 'Do you want some bacon or don't you?'

My anxiety increased because I didn't want any and I was scared she would get more angry if I said no.

On an impulse I said to her, 'No, but I would like a hug', fearing that she would say no. Instead she smiled and hugged me, folding me in her arms. I woke up with her still holding me.

I closed my diary, switched off my torch and snuggled down into my sleeping bag. Life doesn't want us to be frightened and hurting, I thought, as I lay there in the dark, cradled by the earth and soothed by the distant lullaby of the river. This is not what life is about. Life wants us to be whole and fully alive. In fact it needs us: our entire future and the world's future depends upon us healing and becoming whole. So I want to be free – I just don't know how.

One of the things I have realized about the process of growth and transformation is that so much depends upon our intention. It comes back to the principle of what is inside us shaping what happens outside. If we sincerely desire to heal and know the truth then the answers will come, and it is part of the extraordinary grace and synchronicity of life that everything is conspiring with us to help us wake up. The answers may appear in the form of a sudden inspiration, a chance meeting or a slogan on a billboard, but whatever form they take, it is just a matter of time. So even though I didn't know how to heal I trusted that life would show me.

Meanwhile I started thinking about the rest of my life.

I had two major concerns. One was my relationship with Ben. We had split up about six months earlier and I kept wondering if we'd made the right decision. With a new clarity, born of the space and silence in the Grand Canyon, I realized that we had. I remembered when we first met how my intuition told me that we would love each other very much, but that we wouldn't stay together for ever, and reluctantly I accepted that it was time to let go. 'We are limiting each other,' I wrote in my diary. 'We need space to grow and develop, to find out who we really are and what we want in our lives and we can't do that together. Painful as it is now, I feel that in the long run it will be better for both of us.'

And that brought up my other concern: what did I want to do with my life? Although working in television continued to be exciting and my career was flourishing, it didn't satisfy the longing I felt, and that was becoming increasingly important. Again the Canyon gave me ample time and space to think. 'I have no desire to go back to working in TV and yet I don't know what else to do,' I wrote. 'Down here the choices seem very simple. There is a spiritual quality that exerts itself, saying, "This is how you must live; this is the feeling you must create".'

This was quite literally the truth. But it was a deeper lesson than I was able to grasp at the time. For it was teaching me that what I sought would not come simply by changing what I did for a living, but through changing my way of being in the world. That the answer to my soul hunger lay in learning how to connect with the love and joy and wisdom that is the source of our being and in living in daily reverence for the spirit that is present in all things.

In other words I needed to develop my spiritual life. But as I still considered myself to be a diehard atheist, the idea of having a spiritual life was inconceivable, which meant I could only attempt to address my longing by changing what I did. So I went about the business of each day – packing up my tent in the morning, eating peanut-butter sandwiches at lunchtime, sharing a joke or a story with someone – and all the while I was wondering: What should I do?

I was often aware of Roger, the older Frenchman, watching me. He generally sat quietly on his own, apart from the group. One lunchtime I happened to walk close by him, so I stopped.

'What?' I asked him.

He looked perplexed.

'Why are you watching me?'

'Well, you are very beautiful you know . . .'

'Yeah, yeah, never mind the flattery.'

He paused for a moment and then said, 'Because I wish I had your age.'

'But you did have it.'

'Yes,' he replied, a troubled look on his face. 'I did have it. But I was in a concentration camp in my twenties.'

His words shocked me. They made me appreciate more than ever how precious life is. And they made me reflect once again that there are many ways to be imprisoned, from the harrowing captivity of a prison camp to the subtler prisons of the mind.

On the last night I lay on the riverbank listening to the river lapping over the stones and the stones themselves shifting and murmuring. 'I am aware of myself evolving,' I wrote in my diary. 'A chrysalis state is occurring. I am curious and excited about what kind of creature will emerge. I want a greater sense of myself, of solidity and wholeness. I want certainty – not in my life path, but in myself. I want to wake up and draw in deep breaths of satisfaction at being alive.'

From the Grand Canyon I went to visit Joan and Steve in Oregon. To my delight I discovered that William and Jonathon were there too.

'The three of us are going to a workshop this weekend,' Joan explained. 'It's led by someone Jonathon knows and it's about connecting with Spirit. Would you like to come with us?'

'Sure,' I replied, not having the faintest idea of what was involved. 'It sounds like a great idea.'

The workshop was led by a couple called Gary and Christy and it was held at their home, in a remote part of the country outside Portland. It was a beautiful old wooden ranch house on top of a hill, surrounded by trees. Gary was a big bear of a man, with a broad chest and dark, curly hair. Christy was the complete opposite. A tiny wisp of a woman, with long blonde hair and bright, piercing blue eyes, she seemed more angel than human.

In the morning we gathered in their large, vaulted living room and sat in a circle, cross-legged on cushions on the floor. We went round one by one, introducing ourselves and saying why we were there. People talked about wanting to connect with themselves and with God. It all seemed very New Age and strange and the sceptical part of me cringed with embarrassment. When it came to my turn, I said, 'I don't really know why I am here – I came because my family invited me to join them.'

'There are no mistakes,' said Gary with conviction. 'You are here because you are meant to be.'

Inside my soul nodded, so I nodded too, while my inner sceptic stalked off into a corner in disgust.

In the afternoon Christy did healing work with people one-on-one, while the rest of the group watched and supported. 'We all carry emotional wounds,' she explained. 'From childhood and our adult lives. Abandonment, loss, disappointment, abuse – none of us gets through life unscathed. Time passes but the hurt lives on, stored in our bodies as unresolved feelings of pain, grief and anger. The problem is not that challenging things happen, but that we do not know how to respond appropriately to them. We are taught not to feel. At least we are taught to avoid these so-called "difficult" feelings at all costs. Instead we learn to shut down and numb ourselves with work, sex, drugs, alcohol, food. And what is the result? We aren't able to heal and we end up living in constant pain.'

A number of people in the group were nodding in agreement.

'So then,' Christy went on, 'instead of pushing our feelings away we have to learn how to open to them, because not only are they part of life and part of being human, they are vital to the process of healing. You have to feel it to heal it. By expressing our feelings we release them and transformation can happen. The wound heals. Of course it may leave a scar, but this becomes part of who we are, part of the wisdom that we accumulate during our lifetime, part of being whole.

'Now, enough talking – who has something they would like to work with?' A woman put up her hand and said she wanted to heal the pain she felt about her father, who had been an abusive alcoholic. Then one of the men wanted to process the anger and betrayal he felt at his recent divorce. I watched with a mixture of fascination and horror. Here were people openly crying and sharing their deepest hurts, in front of people they didn't even know! After a lifetime of learning never to reveal my feelings or show any vulnerability, I was in shock. Although I had listened attentively to what Christy said, I hadn't understood what she really meant and I certainly couldn't apply it to my own life.

Towards the end of the afternoon Christy asked if anyone else wanted to work on something, and to my astonishment Joan spoke up. 'I want to volunteer Catherine,' she said. She turned to me and explained, 'I think this is a great opportunity for you to work on your mother's death.'

'I agree,' said William.

'Me too,' said Jonathon.

Christy looked at me, an expression of the utmost compassion and gentleness on her face. 'Do you want to, Catherine?'

Did I want to what? I had the unnerving feeling that I was being lovingly encouraged to jump off a cliff, but I agreed anyway. She invited me to lie down and she sat at my head, while the rest of the group gathered around me, touching me gently and holding my hands and feet.

'Tell me what happened,' she said. 'How did your mother die?' I answered as honestly as I could, giving her my reporter-on-the-scene account, my voice flat and emotionless.

'How did you feel?' Christy asked, gently pushing me.

I struggled to answer. 'It's OK, Catherine,' she said, 'you can tell us. How did you feel?'

'Frightened,' I whispered at last.

'Yes,' she said, 'you felt frightened.'

As I lay there I could feel a tremendous shift taking place in my body. My chest was cracking open like the earth's crust as the emotions I had buried for so long began to surface. I fought to keep them under control, to remain calm and composed, but despite my struggle, tears began to trickle down my face.

'Are you still frightened?' Christy asked me.

'Yes,' I answered, battling against my feelings.

'What are you frightened of?'

I couldn't bear to speak. All the years of blaming myself, of feeling guilty and unworthy, made it impossible for me to answer.

'It's OK, Catherine,' Christy reassured me again. 'It wasn't your fault. Let your feelings come. What are you frightened of?'

'I'm frightened that she will be angry with me.' Slowly I managed to choke the words out one at a time. 'That she will blame me for her death.'

'Yes, Catherine, you are frightened she will be angry with you. That she will blame you. What else are you frightened of?'

'I'm frightened that she won't love me any more.' As I said it, my entire body turned to liquid and my grief poured out in deep, wrenching sobs.

Christy and the rest of the group held me quietly as I cried. Eventually my tears stopped and Christy began to speak to me again.

'She loves you so much, Catherine. She is here with us now. Can you feel her?'

'Yes,' I answered.

'Can you see her?'

'Yes.'

'Who else is with her?'

'I am.' Fresh tears began to roll down my cheeks.

'What is she doing?'

'She is holding me by the hand.' Again my voice was choked with sobs.

'Can you feel how much she loves you?'

'Yes.' And I was overwhelmed by another wave of tears.

10. The Light Within

On the second day of the workshop Gary led a guided meditation. We all lay down in the living room and closed our eyes. 'Imagine you are lying down in a meadow high up in the mountains,' he said. 'It is full of flowers and you gaze up at the blue sky, feeling the earth pulse beneath you.'

In fact I didn't see that at all: I saw myself standing on a rocky plateau, the same grey and barren landscape I had seen in my previous vision.

'You get up and walk across the meadow and come to the edge of it,' Gary went on. 'There is a valley far below you with a sparkling river. You want to get to it and you look for a path.'

In my imagination I picked my way painstakingly across the plateau and finally came to the edge, and sure enough I saw a river and a faint path that wound its way down the steep valley side.

'When you get down to the bottom, go into the river.'

Slipping into the water was absolutely blissful. I dipped beneath the surface, caressed by the cool, silky water, aware of my individual being and at the same time indivisible from the river that carried me so effortlessly.

'Look around you,' Gary said. 'On the banks you will see all the world's great teachers, from every religion and philosophy. At any point you can get out of the river and ask their advice. They are here to help you and to tell you whatever you want to know.'

Just as he suggested, the banks gradually filled with figures, some standing on the edge of the shore, others sitting quietly in the shade, some talking to groups of people. Buddha was there; Christ; the Prophet Muhammad. There were Indian saints, Egyptian goddesses and Greek philosophers – teachers and thinkers of every nationality and period in history – and I felt full of awe and appreciation for the wisdom they held.

But I also didn't want to leave the river, where I felt such deep peace and joy, so I drifted on, dipping beneath the surface again. As I did so I noticed the teachers were entering the water, losing their individual form, pouring each inside the other and becoming one with the river. As my own body dissolved I realized that the river was the true source of everything: all wisdom, all love, all joy, all being.

At that moment Gary suggested that we bring the visualization to an end. I knew instantly that the river has no end and even though I was leaving it, it would flow on inside me as my soul. Then Gary invited the group to share their experiences.

'I felt so happy in the river,' I said, when it was my turn, 'that I didn't get out.'

'That's great,' Gary replied. 'The river represents the flow of Spirit and universal wisdom and it is unfolding within us all the time. In essence it is who we are – all we need to do is to remember and learn how to connect with our source.'

I'd love to be able to say that from this point on I got it. That I understood I was on a spiritual journey and I dedicated myself to spiritual inquiry. But the truth is I didn't. Just as the visualization had shown me, I still had a long way to go. And yet at the same time the river was already flowing within me, as it is flowing within all of us. This is the great paradox of being human. The unbounded love, wisdom and truth of our divine nature is not only inside us all along, it is who we truly are but we just don't know it – and this is the point of a spiritual journey. The word 'journey' implies that we have to go somewhere to find what we are looking for, but a spiritual journey is not about going anywhere, it is about turning within to the core of our being and discovering that which has been hidden within us all along. That which we truly are and always have been.

But despite the experiences I'd had in the Grand Canyon and the guided meditation, I returned to England oblivious to the fact that I was on such a journey. Back in London it was December – cold, wet, dark and dismal. After the sunshine and vastness of Oregon and the Grand Canyon, my flat seemed unbearably cramped and tiny, like a doll's house, and I unpacked with a leaden heart, wishing that I could have stayed in America. But without a green card that was impossible, so I stuffed my jeans and hiking boots into the back of my wardrobe and pulled out a shirt and trousers from Joseph and high-heeled boots from Pied A Terre, ready to wear to work the next day.

I had a new job with a company called Wall To Wall TV as an assistant producer on an ongoing documentary series. They were one of the most innovative and cutting-edge independents and supposedly they only hired the best people, so it was something of an achievement to be working for them. But as I trudged through the rain the following morning, the question was still there: Did I really want to?

Christmas and New Year 1991 passed in the usual frantic blur of deadlines. Even so I was struck by how much better I felt inside. Letting go of the guilt and grief I had bottled up about Tate's accident was a huge relief, like putting down something you have carried for so long that it is not until you stop that you realize what an immense burden it has been. And I went around hugging myself with a sense of secret delight, because now I knew what I had suspected for so long: that it is possible to heal the wounds we carry.

That much was fantastic. What wasn't so great was that despite all the time I had taken off work my energy levels were still really low. Through sheer will-power I could force myself to keep going, but I knew that wasn't healthy and I didn't want to risk getting psoriasis again. Joan told me about a healer she saw in Oregon. 'He practises something called "clinical kinesiology",' she said. 'I don't know how it works, but it does. Maybe he could refer you to someone in England.' It turned out that his teacher, Robert Harding, lived in London, so I called him straight away and found myself lying on his treatment table a few days later.

'I use muscle-testing as a form of diagnosis to check the major systems in your body – that way I can ascertain exactly what is working and what isn't,' Robert explained. 'Hold your right arm straight against your body: I am going to pull it away from you and I want you to resist me. Whether you are strong or weak gives me information about what is happening in your body. OK?'

'OK.'

With that he began, hovering around me, muttering unintelligibly to himself, tugging frequently on my right arm, which I was mystified to discover was strong at some moments and completely limp at others. While he worked he asked me questions about my childhood and my life now.

'Overall you are very weak,' he said at last, speaking a language I could understand all too well. 'I can help you, but it is not going to be easy. Your body is under immense strain, your immune system is very depleted and you are not absorbing food properly. This is causing serious deficiencies and in turn these deficiencies compromise many of the body's most important functions. It will take time, patience and a lot of effort on your part to heal. Without your commitment I can't do anything.'

I didn't want it to be difficult. I wanted him to fix me, preferably right now or at least quickly.

'What do I have to do?'

'First of all you have to come to see me weekly.'

'But I'm really busy,' I replied. 'Sometimes I'm away filming, and the rest of the time things are frantic. I don't know if I can make it every week.'

'Then come whenever you can. Secondly you have to be willing to face what comes up. The method I use works on the mind and body as a whole. All the experiences from your life that you haven't been able to deal with are stored in your body. In order to heal, these experiences have to be released. So there will be times when you will feel old emotions like fear and grief surfacing. It can be difficult and painful.'

I hesitated, then nodded. I felt so exhausted I was willing to do anything to get better, and although intellectually I didn't understand what Robert was doing, on a body level I trusted him completely. Soon my sessions with him were like weekly visits to an oasis. I arrived feeling so tense and tight, it was as if I wore an iron cage beneath my skin, clamped around my chest and back. By the end of the session my body and nervous system had unwound and I began to get a taste of how calm and relaxed it is possible to be.

Just as Robert suggested, there were times when old emotions started to release. Sometimes for days after a session I would feel things stirring within me and I had the sense of something dark and rotting floating up to the surface, like toxic waste coming up from the bottom of the ocean. During those times I found myself bursting unexpectedly into tears or having sudden flashes of anger and rage.

'Is it all right?' I asked Robert. 'Sometimes I just don't feel in control.'

'Yes,' he said, concealing a smile, 'it is good. For you, being in control means denying your feelings so that you appear to be fine. Losing control therefore means that you are starting to feel, which is essential in order to become healthy. When emotions like grief and anger get stuck in the body, not only do they cause us terrible pain, eventually they will lead to disease. So we have to learn to express how we feel in an appropriate way – in other words without acting it out and causing hurt or harm to anyone. So let yourself cry when you need to. And if you are feeling angry, pound some pillows or whack the sofa with a cricket bat – it might sound funny, but it works, because it releases the energy in a safe way.'

'I know,' I said. 'You have to feel it to heal it.'

'Quite so,' he replied.

As the months passed I trusted Robert more and more and he continued to ask me questions about my childhood,

Tate's death, my work in television, what I really wanted in my life. With extreme gentleness he helped me begin opening up about things I had never spoken about before. Didn't even know one could speak about. Like my fear of being abandoned. Or the fear of not being good enough.

One day he said, 'Catherine, if you want to get better faster, I strongly encourage you to start therapy. Really, there is only so much I can do on a physical level to help you. As I've explained, the mind and the body are not separate: you have to address both in order to heal. Please think about it.'

'OK,' I said, 'I'll think about it.' Neglecting to mention the fact that I had already been thinking about it for years, because something still held me back.

Instead I worked at Wall To Wall until July and then I escaped to Oregon again, visiting Steve and Joan at their cabin in the mountains. It had been eight years since my first visit and it was just as beautiful as before. The river ran on, sparkling and clear. The trees stretched up into a fabulously blue sky. The cabin was quiet and serene and Joan and Steve were warm and welcoming as ever.

Joan and I spent most of our time hiking, climbing steep trails up to meadows filled with wild flowers and spectacular views of the mountains. 'Let's go to Tam McArthur Rim tomorrow,' she suggested after I had been there for a week or so. 'It's one of my favourite places. It leads right up to the base of Broken Top and it has an amazing view looking out over the Three Sisters. I'd love to show it to you.'

The first part of the trail wound steadily uphill through a pine forest. After an hour we came out of the trees on to a wide plateau, which stretched away to the west. To the south stood Mt Bachelor, a lone mountain skirted by forests and capped with snow, and we stopped for a little while to rest and admire. Then we turned to the west and picked up the path that led along the plateau. There were fresh deer tracks on the trail. 'Yes,' they seemed to say, 'this way, follow us.' And I had the feeling that I was being led towards something unutterably precious. At one point I looked up and saw them leaping ahead of us, a doe with two fauns, their step so light and graceful they appeared to float across the land.

After another hour we came to a short, steep hill and puffed our way to the top and there were the mountains right in front of us. Broken Top was immediately to our left and the Three Sisters stretched away to the right; their magnificent dark slopes, jagged and steep and scattered with patches of snow, were so close it seemed I could reach out and touch them. Their beauty hit me like a blow to the chest, splitting me wide open and my soul soared out in exultation, swooping and gliding through the vastness of the light and air. 'Wow!' I called out to Joan. 'They are so beautiful!' She smiled back, her face brimming with delight.

My whole being was awash with the same boundless joy I had felt in the mountains before. Yes, yes, yes, yes, yes, yes, I remembered, this is what matters! This feeling of awe and reverence. This sense of connecting with that which is infinite and eternal. For I was struck by the power of the mountains. By their abiding presence of strength and stillness and the sense that they were rooted in something much deeper and older than the earth on which they rested. They are witnesses to eternity, I realized. And that is what I want to be: a witness to eternity.

All too soon Joan said it was time to go, and reluctantly I followed her back down the trail. As I walked along I looked at the rocks and stones lying on either side. Occasionally I stopped to pick up a piece, measuring its weight in my hand and feeling the warmth in it from the sun. Some were made of hard, grey, glittery granite. Others, my favourite kind, were made of sandstone, with bands of colour ranging from pale orange to bruised purple, swirled together like a muted rainbow. I could turn the whole experience into poetry and say that the stones were shining with light, but although that would convey what I felt, it would not describe what actually happened. They were simply ordinary stones, lying on the ground, the kind you might walk past every day for a thousand years and not notice, until one day you do. On this day I did.

I saw they really were shining with light, not literally but inherently, shimmering with the same light and power that shone from the mountains. I couldn't have said what this light was, but as I gazed around me at the rocks and trees, I knew it was in everything, no matter how small or humble. And that if it was in everything, it must also be in me! I stood there rooted to the spot as relief and delight flooded through me. In me! In everything! This most mysterious and precious light!

I knew that for the first time I was seeing the world as it really is – imbued with spirit – and in that moment of clear seeing, I suddenly became aware of the limitations of my everyday state of awareness. Poor minds, I thought, they are trained to only think logically and rationally, until we come to believe that if something can't be measured then it doesn't exist and therefore we cannot see the presence of spirit, even though it is right under our very nose. Which means the rational mind can't be trusted to see what is real, and so although it is a brilliant tool, rational or logical thinking is not a good way to try to determine reality. For the true nature of reality cannot be measured or formulated or even described, it can only be known intuitively through a fully open mind.

I set off down the trail. Yet even while my whole being was reverberating with these new insights, my rational way of viewing the world was already reasserting itself. 'Light and beauty indeed,' sneered my inner sceptic, quietly at first, so I could barely hear it, but getting ever louder. 'What utter nonsense. They were just stones!' Immediately the doubts started. Maybe I am making it up, I worried. Or letting myself get carried away by my imagination. With that thought, like a wrestler pulling a sudden move, my rational mind snapped back into place and I was once more in its grip. I looked again at the rocks and trees: now they were just that, rocks and trees. Beautiful of course, but the light had again become imperceptible to me.

Except this time I didn't forget, because I knew that what I had seen and felt was real, even though I couldn't see or feel it any more. So for the first time I became conscious of the split in me between my rational view of the visible world and my intuitive perception of the invisible presence of Spirit. I was so used to trusting this rational way of defining reality that I couldn't just drop it there and then. But nor could I deny the truth of what I had experienced. So the civil war between my ego and my soul began in earnest and for years I would struggle with it, until finally I had to decide which to trust: what I had been taught to believe or what I felt through direct experience to be true.

A couple of days later, Joan and I were out walking again. 'How's the healing work going?' she asked me.

'It's good, Robert has helped me a lot. He is an amazing man, one of the kindest people I have ever met and certainly the wisest.'

'Is your energy better?'

'Yes, but it's still not great. Here I feel OK. The mountains fill me with their vitality. In London and at work I get very depleted. Robert says I should start therapy. That he can't do much more to help me without it.' I stopped there, the implicit question hanging, as if I wanted her permission.

'Does that seem right to you?'

'Well, it makes sense. But I'm scared or ashamed or something. Part of me feels that I shouldn't need therapy, that it is weak and self-indulgent. That I should be strong and hold it all together and just get on with my life.' My voice trembled as I spoke and I felt tears in my eyes.

'Oh Catherine, don't be ashamed,' Joan said, turning round to face me on the trail. 'I think it takes a great deal of courage to look inside and explore what is really going on rather than pretending to be fine. And your life is at stake: you must do whatever you can to become happy and healthy.'

When I finally made it into a therapist's office several months later, it was not because of Tate or my energy. It was because I had been in another editorial meeting at work where I was unable to contribute my ideas because, just as I had been at university, I was still terrified that people would think what I said was stupid. So I was about to make a suggestion when I was silenced by my inner critic. 'You can't say that!' it hissed. 'Do you want everyone to know what an idiot you are?' Then someone else said the very thing I was thinking of and the whole team agreed it was a brilliant idea.

What the hell is going on here? I wondered. How did I come to believe that my ideas are stupid by definition simply because they are my ideas? And why am I so scared? The discussion in the meeting flowed on, but I was preoccupied with my own thoughts. I can't go on sabotaging myself like this, I decided finally. I am going to start therapy. I asked Robert if he could recommend someone. He thought about it for a moment, and then said, 'You could try the Association of Jungian Therapists for a referral or see if there is a counselling centre close to where you live, but the best person I know is my wife, Clare.' If Clare is good enough for Robert, I thought, then I am sure she is good enough for me, so I made an appointment.

I walked into her office feeling very nervous, but was immediately reassured by her presence. She was tall, with long ash-blonde hair, perhaps fifteen years older than me, and her manner was kind and gracious. She welcomed me in, invited me to take a seat and sat down opposite me. She asked me a few basic questions, like how old I was and what work I did, where I grew up, about my family and my current relationship status. Then when she had a general picture, she said, 'OK, so why are you here?'

'Well, I have been thinking about coming to therapy for years, for lots of different reasons,' I replied. 'But in terms of why I am here right now, it's because I notice how I constantly doubt myself, especially at work, and I can't bear it any longer.'

'Can you give me an example?' she asked.

I told her about the recent meeting.

'So what are you afraid of?'

'I am afraid that what I have to say is stupid and therefore I will be humiliated.'

'And where does that fear come from? In order to heal something we not only have to notice that it is happening, we have to deal with the roots of it, by going back into the past to find the place where it originated . . .'

And so we began. I soon discovered that one of the great things about therapy is that no matter where you start it will lead you right to the core problems that need to be healed. Clare helped me see that my difficulty in sharing my ideas was part of my ongoing belief that I was not good enough, and with her help I finally began to unravel where that belief came from and why. The simple act of speaking about what had happened, of naming it and bringing it into consciousness was an immense breakthrough for me and I quickly came to appreciate the value of having a safe place in which to explore what was going on inside.

Clare also taught me skills and techniques that helped me deal with things in a more skilful way. I learnt to track back through time to find the source of the beliefs I held. I learnt to talk to the different and conflicting parts of myself to find out what they wanted and needed. And I learnt how to catch myself and stop just for a moment, so that instead of responding automatically to a situation, I had the chance to ask: What is really happening here and how can I act rather than react? She even had a technique for working with trauma, so that I was no longer plagued by flashbacks of the accident.

I felt as if I were sorting the wheat from the chaff as I sifted and sorted through the incredibly complex charade of thoughts, ideas, beliefs, patterns and experiences I called 'me', to find out which, if any of it, actually was me. And as we worked, I saw more and more clearly that healing and becoming free meant breaking out of my old beliefs and stories in order to discover what was really true.

11. The Business of Dissolving

One day, during one of our sessions, seemingly apropos of nothing, Robert said, 'Catherine, you need to commit to a spiritual path.'

What – me? I thought. A spiritual path? Don't be ridiculous. My contempt for anything to do with God was still so great that the likelihood of me deliberately choosing a spiritual path was zero to none. Yes, I had seen the light that is present in all things, but as far as I was concerned that was just energy and it had absolutely nothing to do with God or spiritual paths.

Of course I didn't express my incredulity out loud or ask Robert why he thought that. I wish I had. Maybe he would have told me the truth. Maybe he would have said, 'Catherine, I know you think you are an atheist, but like it or not, you are on a spiritual journey and one day you will find that out. The only choice you have right now is whether to make it easier for yourself.'

A few months later he tried again. 'Go and see some friends of mine,' he suggested. 'Ronnie and Rachel. They have a weekly group studying the writings of Ibn Arabi. He was a great Sufi teacher, who lived in the Middle Ages. They might help you find what you are looking for.'

'I'm not looking for anything,' retorted the silent but indignant voice of my ego. But while it was busy protesting, my soul nudged me into action and I found myself saying, 'OK, I'll go.'

It turned out that they lived in north London, just round the corner from my friend Tish, so I asked her to come with me and on the following Monday we knocked on their door at 6.30 p.m. Ronnie opened it, greeted us both warmly and showed us into the living room. It was furnished with several slightly battered but comfortable sofas and a number of chairs. There were eight people already there and when Tish and I sat down, the evening began.

First we sat for twenty minutes in silence and meditated. I was curious about meditation and open to the idea of it, but I didn't know how to do it, so I just sat very still and hoped that would do the trick. Then Rachel read out loud from a book. The words were very beautiful and it was full of references to the lover and the Beloved. After that a discussion ensued about the meaning of this passage. People talked animatedly and the phrase 'the veil' was repeated frequently.

'What do you think, Catherine?' Ronnie asked me suddenly.

Think? I didn't have the faintest idea what was going on. So I sat there for a few moments trying to figure out what to say. For once I couldn't come up with an answer. There was only the truth, so I said it. 'I honestly don't understand what you're talking about. What is the veil?' I looked around at everyone. They were all looking at me, especially Tish, who had a particularly mischievous gleam in her eye.

'Good question,' Ronnie replied. 'Who would like to explain to Catherine what the veil is?'

One of the men cleared his throat. 'The veil,' he began, 'is the earth and the whole material or phenomenal world. Our bodies, these chairs, this house, these are all part of the veil. Because the material realm appears to be so solid and real, it deceives us into thinking that this is all there is. That this is the beginning and the end of reality. But that is an optical illusion. The material world is actually a manifestation of God. When you learn to look beneath the surface, you will see the presence of God is immanent in all things. If you look deeper still, one day you might be able to see through the veil of the material world altogether and experience God as transcendent – invisible, intangible, ineffable.'

The rest of the room nodded in appreciation and agreement. I nodded too, but inside the only God I was thinking about was of the 'Oh my God, these people are mad' variety. Finally, after more meditation, the evening finished and Tish and I made our escape. 'It was lovely having you,' Rachel said, as we darted out of the door. 'You're welcome to come back any time.'

'Thanks,' I said, feeling extremely uncomfortable, 'umm, it was very interesting.' With that we fled, racing down the street and around the corner, where we both burst out laughing.

'What on earth was that all about?' Tish gasped.

'I have no idea.'

'What do you mean you have no idea? You were smiling and nodding!'

'Well, what else was I supposed to do? Get up and say, "Sorry, but I think you're all crazy"?'

'So you don't have any idea what they were talking about?'

'None.'

'Good, 'cause neither do I.' And we went home, both satisfied with our own ignorance.

'How did it go?' Robert asked me the next time I saw him.

'Umm . . .' I played for time, while I tried to figure out what to say. 'I guess I didn't really understand what they were talking about.'

'Oh, well that's natural – it's a very different way of seeing the world from the one that you're used to. Will you go back?'

'Umm . . . maybe.'

Of course, I didn't.

Instead, after another year of working crazily, my longing and soul-hunger drew me back to the mountains. Every August Joan and her friend Mary Kate went on a two-week hiking trip to a different set of mountains. It was the core of their friendship and they told wonderful stories about their adventures, sharing the untarnishable treasure of memory: the sunsets, wild flowers, bear sightings, sudden snowstorms and glorious mountain peaks.

That year they were going to the Sawtooth Mountains in Idaho. 'At seventy-one and sixty-eight, Mary Kate and I are too old to carry heavy backpacks any more,' Joan wrote to me in a letter. 'So I have hired a packing company to take care of all the logistics. They will provide us with two cowboys and a team of horses to carry all the food and gear. While we hike during the day, the cowboys ride ahead, set up camp and make dinner. They even cook breakfast, too. Without packs to carry, we can cover ten or twelve miles a day and hike right into the heart of the mountains. Would you like to join us? It would be so lovely if you could come too.'

We arrived at the horse corral early in the morning to drop off our gear and found two young men, nineteen years old at most, strapping coolers and cooking equipment on to three horses. Wearing Stetsons and with cigarettes dangling effortlessly from their lips, they could have walked straight out of a Marlboro commercial. I don't know who was more surprised, them or us, for both boys looked us up and down with an expression of undisguised astonishment. 'We ain't taken ladies out hiking before,' one of them volunteered.

'Oh,' I said, 'what do you normally do?'

'We take men out hunting and fishing.'

'Damn,' said Mary Kate, laughing. 'I forgot to bring my rifle. I guess we'll just have to make do with hiking after all.'

The mountains were utterly gorgeous – steeply sloped granite peaks standing proud against a clear, clear sky. We started on an easy trail winding up through pine trees to a valley, which held the first of many cobalt-blue lakes. We stopped for lunch and Joan and I wandered along the lake's edge, picking up stones, beauty after beauty, showing them to each other with such loving tenderness they might have been as delicate as newborn chicks or valuable as diamonds.

By the afternoon my body was beginning to sing. Waves of happiness and delight rippled through me. The clutter of work and London was cleared from my mind as I was washed clean by the light and brilliance of the mountains. We camped that night by a second lake nestled in a higher valley. After a dinner of fried chicken, gravy and mashed potatoes, we retired gratefully to bed. The stars seemed extraordinarily bright as I lay in my sleeping bag gazing upwards, while my weary body adjusted itself to the unfamiliar hardness of the ground.

The next day as we climbed up to a high pass on the shoulder of a mountain, I stopped to rest and take in the view. In every direction peaks and valleys rolled away in an ocean of impossible beauty. I looked behind me just as Joan came around a switchback and began walking up towards me. Her whole being radiated joy. It was streaming through her, pouring out of every cell. She seemed so small and vulnerable against the vastness of the mountains and yet there she was, living, breathing, shining forth, just like the rocks and trees around her, with the magnificence of Creation. I felt my heart burst with love, for Joan, for the mountains, for everything.

Several days later, we camped by a large lake and decided to stay there for a second night, which gave us a layover day. We were deep in the mountains by this time, and over breakfast the next morning Joan and Mary Kate planned to hike up to a viewpoint overlooking the adjacent valley. I decided to go with them, but as I got ready to leave camp, my intuition said, 'Don't go, wait: something is going to happen.'

I shrugged it off and went anyway, setting off up the trail with my usual eagerness. The cool early-morning air pressed against my skin like water, the scent of the pines was sharp, and I felt the muscles in my legs warm and stretch as the path began to climb. An hour later and the trees had already begun to thin. I stopped to wait for Joan and Mary Kate in a pool of sunshine, my face upturned towards the light, enjoying the vivid contrast of tree and sky. Still the feeling was there. 'Don't go on,' it said, 'come back to the lake, come back.'

Joan and Mary Kate appeared around a turn in the path, their faces happy and smiling, and they sat down beside me to rest. I waited with them until they were ready to go on and then said, 'I'm going back to camp.' I saw a flicker of concern on Joan's face. 'Nothing's wrong,' I added. 'I can't explain why, it's just a feeling I have that I'm meant to be somewhere else today.'

There was no mistaking my destination when I came to it. I walked through our camp and around the lake till I came to a clearing in the trees where a large, flat rock jutted out over the water. I climbed up on to it and sat down. What now? I wondered. I felt certain this was where I was meant to be, so I just sat there with the lake, the birds, the trees, the rock, the light all around me. I sat there and I sat there. Gradually my breath slowed and deepened until it seemed as if I had been turned inside out and I was no longer the one breathing, for the breath was breathing me.

I was so still, not just physically, but mentally. My habitual whirlwind of thoughts and ideas and memories had died down, like sand settling in the bottom of a jar of water, leaving the rest of my mind absolutely clear. I felt a deep sense of calm and peace. I had no need to do anything, no need to prove anything, to fix anything, to figure anything out. I could just be present in each moment, appreciating it for exactly what it was. Noticing with each breath, I am here. I am alive. I am in a world surrounded by life.

So I sat there, breathing, being. And as I sat I heard the short, rapid stroke of wings as some ducks flew over the lake. I heard the skidding of their outstretched feet across the water and I felt the ripples in my own being, as if my body and the body of the lake were one. And like a reflection on still water broken by a stone casually tossed, my sense of myself as a separate being began to disintegrate.

The boundaries of my body dissolved and every cell released the experience of separation as I melted into the rock beneath me. I was no longer disconnected from the world around me, no longer shut off or apart from the rest of life. Instead I just existed as a rock or a tree exists, as a bundle of energy assembled in a particular form. Each created thing individual and unique yet also the same, part of the whole and indivisible from it, just as a single leaf is indivisible from the whole tree and a tree is indivisible from the earth.

Up to that point I had thought I was experiencing the world – thought I was seeing, hearing, feeling, participating in reality – but now it became more real, like waking up from a dream. I realized that most of the time I did not experience reality directly. Instead, just as a window-pane separates us from the greater world outside the little rooms in which we live, I was separated from reality by my mind and its constant stream of thoughts. And by my ego, my sense of identity and the belief that 'I' existed as something separate from the rest of life.

As I sat there on that rock, the window-pane dissolved and for the space of an afternoon, my sense of I, Catherine, ego, maker of television programmes, daughter of Cyril, owner of flat and cat, and the whole structure of my personality melted away. I had no thoughts, no chatter, no planning, no memories, no voices, no likes or dislikes, no running commentary about what was happening, no me. Nothing but the experience of being. Nothing but the experience of merging into the oneness of life.

By the time I had the impulse to get up it was almost

dark. I wandered back to the camp, dazed and full of awe. Joan and Mary Kate looked at me questioningly and then at each other. But they said nothing and I was relieved because I couldn't possibly have explained what had happened to me. I knew it was a continuation of the experience I'd had in Oregon the previous summer. When I saw the light and beauty that is in all things, I had realized intellectually that everything comes from that light and that therefore everything is one. Now that knowing had shifted from an intellectual awareness to a direct experience of the oneness of all things.

But what that meant or what I was supposed to do with it I couldn't say, because I genuinely didn't know. Like giving a book to someone who cannot read, I didn't know how to understand this experience. Amazing and wonderful as it was to feel at one with everything, I couldn't see how it applied to my ordinary life. 'Well,' said my ego, summing up my predicament, 'this dissolving and merging business is all very good, but you can't earn a living doing that.' And that was still my primary concern. Over the previous few days I had become more painfully aware than ever how unsatisfying my life in London really was. But because I still didn't realize that what I was seeking would require a shift in my whole way of being and understanding the world, I still thought I could solve my dissatisfaction by changing my career. And with that thought my state of consciousness contracted and I was back behind the window-pane, back in the story of my little, separate self.

A few days later we left the mountains and I flew back to England. I wished more than ever that I could stay in America, but there was still the problem of a visa. My father had discovered that as a result of his marriage to Vicki I was eligible for a green card. But the application was taking ages to process and there was no guarantee about when it would come through. So I dragged myself on to the plane, comforting myself with the thought that one day, if I wanted to, I would be able to stay in America permanently.

It is often said that everything happens at the right time, in the right order, and I believe that is true. For much as I wanted to stay in America, I realize now that there was actually a lot that I needed to learn and sort out in England before I was ready to go anywhere. And as I had discovered at university, you cannot leave your problems behind you, so the only real way out is through.

I got back to England in August and started work on a series of films about homelessness for Channel 4. One day while I was researching in Bristol, I heard about a man called Tony, who volunteered for Shelter. He collected food that had passed its sell-by date from several of the local supermarkets and then drove around at night delivering it to places where he knew he would find homeless people. He also had blankets, matches and a limited supply of cigarettes, the most sought-after item of all.

We met in a little café on a rainy afternoon and after talking for a while he invited me to join him on his round that night. At the end of the evening, he took me to meet a man called John. 'You'll like him,' Tony said, 'he's a lovely man.' We drove off to the outskirts of the city and parked outside a dark and derelict building. 'Wait here,' Tony said, 'I'll go in first and see if he'll talk to you.' Moments later Tony waved to me from the broken doorway. 'Don't sit down and don't touch anything,' he warned as we went in. 'And be careful, it's pitch black in there.' I went in through the door, holding on to Tony's arm, and within two steps I was in complete darkness. As we walked into a second room the stench hit me like a wall and I had to resist the impulse to bend over and throw up.

'You're here then?' A voice spoke to us out of the darkness and I heard the scrabble of a hand with matches and then there was the bright flare of light. John was lying on the floor and the light from the match in his hand bounced up, highlighting his ravaged and craggy face. He struggled to light a stump of candle and the match went out, plunging us into even deeper darkness. Then a second flare, and this time the candle flickered into life, a small, dim flame throwing crazy shadows across the walls.

I let go of Tony and walked closer to John. The floor was covered in a thick layer of rotting newspaper and plasterboard that had fallen down from the ceiling. It was mushy beneath my feet and I shuddered to think what else I was treading on. I crouched down, looked into John's eyes and said hello. Gazing back at me across the candle flame was one of the most noble faces I had ever seen.

He was quite drunk, but still articulate, and it was clear he was well educated. He talked of places he had travelled to and philosophized about the world and his condition. 'People don't talk to me,' he said. 'No. I say hello to them, but they won't talk to me. They see the bottle I suppose and . . . Well, it's understandable, isn't it? One can understand why they don't want to talk to me, can't one?'

I nodded. One could understand it all too well, and I thought regretfully of all the times I had walked past homeless people and looked away.

'Still,' he went on, 'it makes it very lonely. I am not a bad person you know, even though I have ended up like this.'

As I listened to him speak, it struck me that the desire to be acknowledged is a universal need – the need to be seen for who we truly are. Of all the hardships homeless people complained to me about – being cold, hungry and scared – it was the feeling of being invisible they found hardest to bear. Each time someone spoke to me about this I felt deeply moved, and I often found myself saying, 'I see you. I hear you. I understand.' And I did, because in the way that life is a mirror always showing us our own reflection, they were showing me my own desire to be seen for the real me.

When the research period was over, I teamed up with a director called Coky and we went back to Bristol and interviewed John. The lights for the camera revealed the true horror of the place where he slept. Rubbish lay rotting in heaps and there were piles of shit all over the floor. But despite the poverty and the awful surroundings, John retained a dignity and a degree of self-awareness that was truly remarkable.

'You won't find me despondent,' he said during the interview. 'I don't cry about my state. I accept the bad times and I know what this is doing to me,' he pointed to his bottle of cheap sherry. 'It's killing me, isn't it? Isn't it?'

A few weeks later I was in the office when Tony rang. 'I've got some bad news,' he said. 'John is dead.' I put down the phone, told Coky and we both cried. Oh well, I thought, at least we can pay him tribute. At least we really saw him, even if it was just for a moment.

When the homelessness series was broadcast on Channel 4, it was a huge success and I felt privileged to have been a part of making it. Then I moved on to another job and found myself working with an old friend called Liz, so one day instead of working straight through, we did something extremely radical and went out to lunch. As we walked back to the office we were having the usual conversation about how unbelievably stressful and awful television was, and wondering why we did it.

'Do you ever think about what it would be like to be on the other side of the camera?' Liz asked. 'To be an interviewee, to have something that you wanted to talk about, something about which you felt really passionate?' Deep inside me, I had the unsettling feeling that my soul was lifting its head, as if it had finally waited long enough.

'I wonder,' I answered her, brushing the feeling aside. 'What would you talk about?' But really I was asking myself that question. What would I talk about? More to the point, would I dare to? The mere prospect of being interviewed triggered an instant rush of fear. I guess that's why I'm behind the camera, I thought, noticing the feelings of panic – because that way I can stay hidden.

'The trouble is,' I said to Clare, as I told her about the conversation with Liz in my next therapy session, 'I'm still so ashamed of being me.'

'This is something that we all have to work with,' she replied. 'As you know, when we are children we develop a persona and cover up the parts of ourselves that we think are bad or unacceptable in order to try and win love, approval and security. It's a good survival strategy, but the risk is that we spend our entire lives pretending to be who we think we ought to be, because we believe we are not good enough or lovable the way we really are.'

'But that's just it,' I said. 'I'm sick of pretending and feeling ashamed. I want to be me. When I think of all the homeless people I met who so desperately wanted to be seen, it's clearly a fundamental human need to be loved and valued for who we really are.'

'Yes, it is. But in order to be seen we have to show who we really are, which means stripping away the masks and layers of pretence. It is about individuating and becoming authentic, and that isn't easy. It's also a process and it doesn't just happen overnight.'

'And it's also completely terrifying,' I said. 'It's like getting naked. Only it's a lot more revealing than taking your clothes off.'

'Yes,' said Clare laughing, 'it's exactly like that. But you have to remember that fear is not the same thing as the truth. Just because you were judged in the past doesn't mean that who you are or what you think is wrong or stupid, or that the whole world will judge you in the same way. So even though letting go of the persona is scary, it is so worth it, because it means we can stop living a lie and stop judging and hating ourselves for being who we really are. Which in turn allows us to accept and appreciate other people for who they are.'

The more we worked together the more I came to trust that I didn't have to pretend or hide with Clare, because she had no judgement about who I was or how I should be. My time with her each week gave me a safe space for the real me to come creeping out. I shared my thoughts and ideas, my dreams, my doubts, my deepest fears, and she made them all welcome. It was the same uncondi-tional love and acceptance that I felt from Robert, from my cousins in Oregon, from the mountains and the earth, from life itself. It was a love that said, 'Yes, I see you, I love you, I want you to be here fully, exactly as you are.'

I now know that we all need this kind of love – the invitation and permission to become who we really are. Initially it has to come from the outside, but in the end we have to learn how to give it to ourselves. And I began learning to accept myself, the whole of myself, with all the different parts of my personality, both good and bad. And at the same time I kept searching for the real me. Who am I, really? I asked myself, over and over again. Little suspecting that this question would eventually take me beyond the boundaries of my personal self and into that great unsayable something that is the source of everything.

12. Getting Naked

Despite the fact that I was still uncertain whether I wanted to work in television, my career was thriving and in the summer of 1994, Jane, the head of Wall To Wall TV, asked me to produce a series for BBC2 called *Slice of Life*. It was a big promotion. I had produced single documentaries before, but never a series, and I was flattered to be offered it. All my friends and colleagues were suitably impressed and my father wrote to congratulate me and tell me how proud he was of my achievements.

On the outside I basked in the glory of all this long-sought-for approval, but inside I was having serious doubts, because my intuition told me not to do it. I knew that the consequences of going against my instinct could be serious, but I was in a quandary. It was all very well for my intuition to say no, but what was I supposed to do instead? How was I going to support myself? What was I going to do with my life? There were no clear instructions about that.

The idea for the series was to tell the social history of post-war England through the story of food. There were six films, each covering a decade. The first explored rationing and the impact of the Second World War. The second was about the perfect housewife and the expansion of the middle class in the 1950s. The third told the story of how English culture opened up to style and pleasure and sex through the arrival of American-style coffee bars and the boom in travel to the Mediterranean. The fourth looked at immigration and racism, through the story of the Indian restaurant, and so on . . .

As I talked through the schedule and budget with Jane, it seemed very tight to me, but as I had never produced an entire series before, I allowed her to persuade me it would be OK. 'We just need very experienced directors,' she said. 'People who really understand how to craft a film – not just because the schedule's tight, but because it's such complicated storytelling.' We discussed a list of suitable candidates and I left it with Jane to contact them. 'Don't worry,' she reassured me as I left her office, 'I'll get really good people.' But I was worried and I arranged to have lunch with a friend, who was a much more ex-perienced producer. He looked at the budget and laughed. 'Don't do it,' he said. 'It's impossible, it will just be a nightmare.'

When I went back for my next meeting with Jane, she told me all the directors we'd thought of had turned it down. 'They all want too much money,' she explained. So instead she had hired two young people from the BBC. 'They are very promising,' she assured me. 'They just don't have much experience.'

'But it won't work,' I said, 'the edit simply isn't long enough for an inexperienced director . . .'

'That's why I am so glad you are producing it,' she interrupted. 'You're brilliant at structuring films and if you oversee each of the edits then you'll be able to keep it on schedule. Anyway, it's part of a producer's job to bring on and encourage young directors . . .'

At that point I didn't need my intuition to tell me not to do it: plain common sense would have been enough.

But there was another reason why I wanted to take the job. Clare practised a form of therapy called neurolinguistic programming, which is an intimidating name for something that is actually very simple to understand and easy to use in everyday life, and I wanted to learn more about it. One day Clare suggested that I take the NLP training course and my intuitive response was a clear 'yes'.

I found out there was a course starting in the autumn, consisting of a four-day weekend once a month, for five months. As a freelance producer/director it was impossible for me to commit to a schedule like that because I never knew where I would be or if I would have the time. By accepting the job as series producer, at least I knew that I would be in London. Whether I would have the time was another question, but I decided to sign up for the course anyway and I negotiated the days off work as part of my contract with Jane.

The first weekend came about a month into *Slice of Life*. We met in a large and rather bland conference room in a hotel in west London. There were about fifty people, mostly from the business and corporate training world, and I looked around me at the suits and ties, wondering if I had made a mistake. But as soon as our trainer, Jim, started speaking I knew I was in the right place.

'First of all I want to give you a sense of how NLP can work for you,' he began. 'As we go through life attempting to understand and make sense of our experiences, we create a set of beliefs about the way life is – that life is hard, for instance, or that you can't trust people, or that you have to give up your dreams. These beliefs become our version or map of reality. Then we operate on the basis of our maps, instead of reality itself. But the map is not the territory and when we mistake the two we shut ourselves off from our own potential and the limitless possibilities of life. The more clearly we see the internal map we hold and how that determines our sense of what is possible, the more we are free to make conscious choices and create the life that we want. That is the power of NLP – the techniques you will be learning over the next five months will enable you to discover what you really want and how to create it.'

Thank God, I thought, sinking back into my chair – that is my question precisely: What is it that I really want? And from that moment I gave the NLP training my un-divided attention. At the end of the first weekend we were asked to select a project. 'Choose something you want to work on, something you want to bring into your life,' Jim said. 'You don't have to decide now. Your first assignment is to think about it and write down what it is you want, using the list of questions provided.' As people gathered their things to leave, they were all buzzing with ideas about what to choose. Quite a few people wanted to give up smoking. One woman wanted to learn to play the piano, and I overheard a man saying that he wanted to spend more time with his children. I already knew what I wanted: to clarify my direction in life.

It was obvious to me that I had reached a crossroads. I could continue working in television. I could change career completely. My new boyfriend Tom wanted us to get married and start a family. And I was still waiting to see if my visa for the States was going to come through. There were so many options facing me, but I didn't know how to choose. Thanks to the initial NLP training I was more aware of the map I held and how my expectations about my future and about things like success and money were leading me in a certain direction. But was that really what I wanted? Underneath all the uncertainty was the persistent longing and the feeling that I was meant to be doing something else. And there was a growing sense of urgency. My intuition was starting to whisper to me, 'Come on, come on, trust me, let me guide you.'

I sat down at my desk one Sunday afternoon to write about my project, and something completely unexpected happened. The world around me faded away somehow: the walls of my room, the window and the garden beyond were still there, but they had receded into the background. Above me was a glowing golden figure, surrounded by a radiant light. At first I thought I was being visited by an angel, and my immediate reaction was, Oh no, this can't be happening to me! But then I realized it was not an angel, it was me, at least it was the essence of me – my soul or true self. The light was bright and clear, flowing through me and around me, so that my whole being was made from it, just as we are all truly made of this light.

Yes, I thought, that is what I want, that light, that radiance – more than anything else, that is what I want. The vision faded and I looked back down at the page of questions. What do you want? the first one asked.

'I want to clarify my direction in life,' I answered.

Why is this important?

'Because at the moment there are many different directions in which I could go and I don't know how to choose. I need to create balance between my life and my work. But more than that, it is finally dawning on me that I need to develop my spiritual life. There is a sense I get sometimes of the light and beauty that is in all things and I want to know how to live my life in alignment with that.'

Do you ever feel like this in the present?

'Yes,' I wrote, 'when I am in the mountains and feeling connected to the whole of life. And through the things I love, from people to a piece of wood or stone . . . Or when I gain insight into myself or a situation.'

What are you going to do in order to get it?

'In order to clarify my direction in life I need to understand what is really important to me and what I want to achieve. So I need to assess the choices I have and order them in terms of value, priority and timescale. I also need to look at the expectations I have about my future. These feelings terrorize me and I want to free myself of them.'

Our projects were evaluated during the course of the next session by one of the training staff, a man called Alan, who gave us feedback and support.

'So you want clarity and greater understanding?' he said. 'And you want to live in alignment with the light?'

I nodded and then said, 'Is it possible?'

'Yes,' he replied, smiling, 'in about ten years.'

But I didn't mean, could I do it? I meant, did it exist, this golden light? Because I still didn't understand what it was or even fully trust that it was real. The next time I went to see Robert I told him about it. 'Yes,' he said, 'that is what we all want.' But he didn't say what the light was either, and I didn't ask.

I had plenty of other questions to worry about, because things at work were not going well. We were just over two months into the schedule and already my worst fears had been confirmed. One of the directors, Ellen, had finished her first film and although it turned out really well, as I had predicted she overran the edit by several weeks. The other director was so inexperienced that after a month Jane and I had to take him off the project completely, which left me with a half-made film to finish and searching for someone to replace him. The expense of losing a director and overrunning the schedule blew the budget out of the water, and on top of handling everything else, I spent hours with the production manager, trying to figure out how we could produce more time and money from nowhere.

By comparison the NLP trainings were like going on holiday. For four days a month I left the insane asylum and entered a world where I felt happy and excited and connected to myself. During the second weekend Jim talked about the role of internal dialogue. 'We all have a host of different parts inside us, with conflicting needs and opinions,' he explained. 'So it is important to be aware of "who" is talking at any given time and what that part's particular agenda is. Maybe it's the internalized voice of your father saying you must do this . . . Maybe it's the voice of your inner child, afraid to stand up for herself and say no in case she is punished. Or perhaps it's the voice of your ego, arguing for what is safest and/or what will make you look good.

'Often this internal dialogue can play out indefinitely, keeping us in a state of "Should I? Shouldn't I?" paraly-sis. So as well as knowing who is talking, we need to know who decides. Which part of you is it that makes the final decision? And is that part serving you? Because that's what we are really interested in – how to make deci-sions that are best for you.'

So the discussion moved on from internal dialogue to

how to make conscious decisions. It was a revelation for me. It made obvious the conflict between my rational mind and my intuition, and when I thought about this in the context of how I made decisions, I realized that I was used to letting my rational mind be the deciding factor. Hence accepting the jobs on *Rough Guides* and *Slice of Life*. Now I realized that I could choose to make decisions in a different way – by trusting my intuition, for example.

At the end of the weekend we were given another project sheet to fill in. What is your project now? it asked.

'My project is still to find clarity and direction in life,' I answered. 'I realize that means opening myself to the "light" that I described previously. I want to find a way of learning how to live in alignment with it. Of incorporating it in my life, and I guess I do mean quite literally embodying it, so that it can flow through me. But I don't know how to handle it or what to do with it. I feel this light, whatever it is, is very powerful. It is both a gift I feel unworthy of and a responsibility I don't know how to carry out. I want to know.'

By that time it was December and I was working twelve- and sometimes fourteen-hour days, six days a week. When I wasn't at work, I thought about the series constantly. Whether I was driving home, lying in the bath, eating breakfast, or awake at three o'clock in the morning, my mind raced with different ideas and possibilities. From how to reorganize the schedule and how to solve any one of a dozen different structural problems in each of the films, to how to design the opening titles for the series and what kind of music to commission.

The whole thing was so challenging, I felt as if I was

on the rack, slowly, slowly, slowly being stretched to breaking point by the pressure and responsibility. Resting or relaxing was out of the question, and I was so anxious I was barely sleeping at all. Christmas came around, with invitations to go to parties and see friends, but I was too busy and too exhausted to see anyone or do anything. Not surprisingly my boyfriend, Tom, began to complain. 'Even when I do see you, you're like a zombie,' he said, as I was lying in bed with him one morning after another night of no sleep. 'What's happened to my girlfriend?' His voice was full of genuine concern. 'I used to go out with this beautiful, funny, vibrant woman, and she's disappeared. Do you know where she's gone?'

'Yes, she's gone to work,' I replied sarcastically, as I dragged myself out of bed.

Thanks to my sessions with Clare I had made good progress in terms of my self-confidence: I was far more comfortable sharing my ideas and trusting my judgement. But I still worried that I wasn't doing enough at work, and I pushed myself to work harder and harder. As I went through the third NLP weekend, I realized how absolutely crucial this issue still was for me. There I was, working fourteen-hour days, and I still didn't know if I was working hard enough! Bloody hell, I thought, it's the same old problem. It all boils down to the belief that I'm not good enough: that's why I'm such a perfectionist, because I'm always trying so desperately hard to prove that I am lovable. I reminded myself, for the five-thousandth time, that my belief was just a story and not the truth, wondering if I would ever be really free of it.

For the third stage of our NLP project we were asked: What is the next step? 'I realize that gaining clarity will take time,' I wrote. 'So it's a question of giving myself time to grow and change. I can now see that I'm used to making decisions with my rational mind and ego, not my intuition or my soul, and that changing this pattern is key. Stress and relaxation are also big problems for me. When I'm tense it's hard to even hear my intuition or soul voice above the general cacophony of internal dialogue, argument and self-doubt. So learning something like yoga or meditation would really help. But right now I'm so busy at work I don't have the time to take on anything else, even something that would be good for me. Therefore I guess my next step is to finish this job and then see what feels right.'

The final NLP weekend was at the end of January. Things were so hectic at work that I had to miss Thursday and Friday morning. By the time I arrived in the training room I was completely frazzled and on the brink of tears. People gathered around me, full of concern.

'What's the matter?' they asked. 'Has something terrible happened?'

'No,' I answered. 'Only work!'

Although I brushed it off, privately I was shocked by their reaction, for their concern forced me to see what a dreadful state I was in, and during the afternoon tea break I studied myself carefully in the bathroom mirror. I had bags under my eyes, my face was drawn and pale, and I looked utterly exhausted. Oh shit, I thought, I can't go on like this.

On the last afternoon we had to get into pairs and explain what our project was and say how we planned to implement it. I paired up with an older man called Victor. He went first and told me he had been using the NLP tools to help him develop a new side to his engineering business and he committed to putting it into action within the next three months.

'What about you?' he asked, when it came to my turn. 'What's your project?'

I gulped. If I could have run away, I would have. 'Well, it is a little hard to say,' I replied. 'I'm not even sure there are words for it. Initially my project was to clarify my direction in life and learn how to choose what is right for me. But I am starting to realize that's got something to do with letting in the light.' I felt utterly ridiculous as I said it: my heart was pounding and I squirmed around in my chair, feeling horribly ashamed.

'Letting in the light . . . ?'

'Um, yes – I mean, the light, the power, the love that is all around us. I don't know how else to explain.'

'Can you show me what it is like when you let the light in?'

'No way!' I replied, horrified by the prospect.

'Why?'

'I'm far too embarrassed.'

'Please try,' he encouraged me. 'I won't tell anyone else, I promise.' And he sat back, waiting patiently.

So I did. I simply looked at him and let the light and the love and the fullness of being flow through me unhindered, as if I had drawn back a pair of curtains, so that the morning sunshine could flood through.

'I see,' said Victor, after several moments. He leant towards me in his chair. 'Catherine,' he said, very serious and sincere, 'that is so beautiful. I feel as if you have just shown me your soul. It's as if you got naked without taking any of your clothes off. Deep down, I think we all want to do that, but we are too shy or something, like we need permission to be who we truly are. You could help a lot of people, just by letting them know that it is OK.'

I felt elated, not knowing whether to laugh or cry. Someone had seen me, seen the light in me, and I hadn't died.

'What will you do next?' he asked.

'I'm not sure. I don't know what this means in terms of how I will actually live my life. Right now my intuition seems to be my only guide, so I guess I have to learn how to listen to it.'

Towards the end of *Slice of Life*, Tom invited me to the seventieth birthday party of a family friend. I knew it was a special occasion and I thought that if I went it might be a way of making up to him for all the times recently I had been working or simply too tired to do anything.

The party was held in a private room at a very smart restaurant in St James's, and so I made a point of dressing up. I wore a black velvet dress and the pair of crystal earrings that I had found all those years ago, when Bon and I were sorting through Tate's things after she died. Just as they had then, the earrings glittered and sparkled, and I could still feel her life-force in them.

As I put them on I could feel her presence with me more strongly than ever and also the ways in which I am like her, so much her daughter that strangers have recognized me and introduced themselves as friends of hers from long ago. She loved parties, loved the opportunity to shine and captivate, and so I made a huge effort to rouse myself from exhaustion and be charming, just as she would have been. The party finished around ten, then Tom and his family suggested we all have dinner, but I pleaded exhaustion and went home.

A year or so earlier I had sold my flat with a view to buying another in a more central part of London. In the meantime I had moved in with a dear friend called Sophia and when I got home from the party, she was sitting downstairs at the kitchen table wearing her pyjamas and drinking a cup of bedtime tea. We chatted for a while before I staggered off to bed, and as we talked I took off Tate's earrings and put them on the table in front of me.

When I woke up the next morning, my first thought was that I must put the earrings away, so I went downstairs to get them, but they weren't there. Perhaps I was so tired that I'd put them away without remembering, I thought, so I went back to my room and checked in their box. It was empty. I checked on my dressing table. I checked on the shelf in the bathroom. I checked the kitchen table again, taking everything off, including the tablecloth. I checked under the kitchen table. They weren't there.

After I had looked in the obvious places, I searched the entire house in a desperate attempt to find them. I even rang Sophia at work, to ask her if she had moved them, borrowed them, thrown them away, destroyed them by accident, anything . . . 'I don't care what happened,' I said, 'just so long as I know.' But she promised me she hadn't touched them. Soon it was eleven o'clock and I forced myself to leave for work, but when I got home again that evening I searched the entire house again, without success.

The next morning, in order to preserve what was left

of my sanity, I got up and went straight to work. That night I came home exhausted and decided that rather than waste more energy looking, I would go to bed, draw my attention inside, still my mind and invite the earrings to show me where they were. I expected to see them tucked behind the bathroom mirror or brushed underneath the sofa, 'invisible' yet obvious. Instead Tate appeared. Her arm was stretched out in a taunting way towards me, the earrings dangling from her fingertips. 'Look what I've got,' she seemed to say.

I was stunned. I lay in bed, completely breathless, as if someone had hit me. I couldn't imagine why she would want to take the earrings, unless she was still angry with me after all this time. Then the very idea that she had taken the earrings at all seemed ridiculous, let alone physically impossible. So I decided the image was just a projection of my own guilt and the feeling that I didn't deserve to have or wear her earrings.

The next morning I woke up determined to find them. I set about an inch-by-inch search of the house. When I had finished looking in all the places they could possibly be I started searching all the places they couldn't. Sometime mid-morning Sophia came home to find me lying on the floor ransacking the back of the cupboard under the stairs.

'What are you doing, Catherine?' she asked.

'I'm trying to find my earrings,' I replied, controlling my anger and tears as best I could.

'How do you think they could have got into there?' she asked innocently. Getting no answer to that, she tried a different approach. 'Shouldn't you be at work by now?'

'Soph,' I said, emerging bottom-first from the cupboard,

'right now I don't give a damn about work, all I care about is finding my fucking earrings.'

'Ahh,' she said, and wisely retreated.

I heard her clomp down the stairs and stop in the middle of the kitchen. 'Catherine!' she shouted. 'Come quickly!' I ran down and she was pointing at the table. There were the earrings, exactly where I had left them on Monday night.

'I promise I didn't put them there,' she said hastily.

'I almost wish you had,' I replied. 'It would make much more sense than what I think has actually happened.' And I told her about the image of Tate.

'Goodness,' Sophia said, surprised but undaunted. 'My granny's talked about that sort of thing happening. You know she's very into psychic phenomena. She says it's called an "à porte". From the French verb porter – to carry.'

'Oh, really?' I answered, thinking things were getting crazier by the minute.

In a daze, I walked slowly back upstairs with the earrings, put them in their box, got dressed and drove to work. On my way there I realized I was already under such pressure from *Slice of Life* that I simply didn't have the energy or the emotional resources to deal with anything else. So I put the whole thing on one side and made a mental note to go and see Robert about it when *Slice* was over.

By the last month of production I was so exhausted that I was in or on the verge of tears the entire time. I woke up in the morning and cried. I walked into the edit and cried. I got home, crawled into bed, and cried. Hell is not a place that exists outside us, I realized, lying awake at three o'clock one morning, too tired to cry. It isn't somewhere we go when we're dead, it's a state of being and this is it. This life I have created for myself is hell.

One day, a couple of weeks before the end, I simply had to get outside, so I went for a walk at lunchtime. It was a cold February day. A bitter wind blew in sharp gusts, whirling dead leaves and litter against a dull grey sky. I hunched my shoulders and stomped along the streets, lamenting to myself about the state of my life. I had hardly slept in months. I'd had several bouts of flu – one of which had turned into bronchitis because I couldn't take time off to rest. The iron cage of tension beneath my skin gripped me more tightly than ever and my stomach was so knotted I could barely eat. Tom and I fought continually about the fact that I was always at work, and it felt like years since I had seen any of my friends. Surely, I thought to myself, work does not have to be like this? Surely, life does not have to be like this?

On my way back to the office I crossed over a busy main road and as I stepped out on to it, a chill ran down my spine. What if I were run over right now? the question came to me; What if I died like this? It wasn't the prospect of death that frightened me. It was the prospect of dying in such a dreadful state. I wanted to die satisfied inside. I wanted to die knowing that I had been fully alive. Knowing that I had discovered who I really am. And that I had lived with as much love as possible. How can I be sure I don't die like this? I wondered. The answer came back loud and clear and devastatingly simple: Change the way you are living.

13. Surrender

'I am thirty years old,' I wrote in my diary in August 1995, sitting once more on the bank of the river Metolius. 'I've left my life in London to find something. It's a soul thing, and what that means I'm not exactly sure. What I do know is that my old life is not letting me grow in the direction that I need, and I am haunted by the feeling that I should be doing something else. In quiet moments this still, small voice opens up inside me. "Come on, come on," it says, "we are losing time."

'"To do what?" I ask, wanting to know in advance.

'But apparently it doesn't work that way, because all this voice – I believe it is the voice of my soul – will say is, "Trust me, I will guide you . . ."

'Whatever it is, now is the time to find out. I could bury myself in some other distraction, a new job in TV, a new career, marriage and a family, but no matter what I did I would just wash up at the same place a little further on down the line. This is something that I can't avoid. It is about aligning myself with my soul and my spiritual path. And my soul is already there, waiting with infinite patience and impatience. I know it can wait for longer than I can. I am like a fish on a line, fighting the inevitable. So I have decided to surrender. "Reel me in," I have said, "show me the way . . ."'

★

When *Slice of Life* finished at the end of April I lay coma-
tose in bed for a week and did nothing. When I finally
summoned the energy I went to see Robert. It had been
months since my last appointment and I arrived in his
office looking like one of the walking dead. 'Oh,' he
said, his eyes scanning me, 'this one has been really bad,
hasn't it?'

Lying on his treatment table I told him about Tate and
the earrings. 'Perhaps she is trying to tell you something,'
he suggested. 'Would you like to know?'

'Yes,' I said, somewhat hesitantly, still scared that she
might accuse me of killing her.

'Then you should call Heddie,' he replied, 'a friend of
mine who is a psychic. She lives near Manchester, so it's
quite a trek. But it's worth it. She's very good.'

I don't know what I expected, but Heddie turned out
to be a tiny old Italian lady, living with her husband in a
very ordinary terraced house, surrounded by family photo-
graphs and old-fashioned china ornaments. She sat me
down and said, 'Have you come about your health?'

'I'm not really sure what I have come for,' I said. 'But
if you have something to tell me about my health, go
ahead.'

'You are getting terribly ill,' she replied. 'Dangerously
ill. It is very, very important that you learn to look after
yourself. You must rest and replenish your system with
the vitamins and supplements it needs and give yourself
time to heal. We will talk about exactly what you need
to take later.

'First, let us look at the rest of your life. Oh, my dear,'
she said, after a moment's consideration, 'you are going
in the wrong direction. You are trying to fulfil someone

else's expectations, not yours. You came to this earth to polish a facet of the beautiful jewel that is your soul. But you are not achieving what you are predestined to achieve because you are trying to please others. You are doubting yourself. Saying, "What shall I do?" Letting yourself be confused by the indoctrinations of someone else.

'Am I making any sense?' she asked.

'Absolutely,' I replied, laughing and crying with the relief of being understood, 'you are describing my life perfectly.'

'So you must give yourself time to reassess, to realize what you are truly made of and what you came to this earth to do. I wish I could tell you what it is,' she went on, reading my mind, 'but it is you who must find out. All I can do is to tell you about your potential. You have a very old soul, very beautiful – you have no idea. You can be a great reassurance and help to many people. But first you have to become sure yourself. You must learn to see God in everything, not God from the Bible, but God the architect that is in all things.

'Right now your pathway is in the penumbra. You are caught in your own shadow – it is making you confused, making you doubt yourself. This is part of your journey. We are all on an endless journey. We are all endeavouring to progress in enlightenment step by step, so that one day we can become the Angels of Light – the Illuminati. It is the journey back to God and it is an uphill spiral.

'So, now you must stop and ask yourself: Who am I really? And where am I going? What can I do that would be truly worthwhile? You have to say, "I am in command and I owe it to my higher self to do what I came to this earth to do."' For such a tiny and elderly lady her voice was strong and emphatic, ringing with the rich, dramatic tones of her Italian accent.

'But how will I know what is right?'

'You will feel it. You will feel what is right. And then you must do it no matter what other people say. If they say, "Stop!" and yet you truly feel that it is the way to do something worthwhile, then that is the way you must go, even if you have to go through hell to get there.'

Towards the end of the interview Heddie asked me again why I had come. I was reluctant to specifically mention Tate, because I wanted to see if Heddie had anything to say about her unprompted. So I started to say it was about someone who had died. 'No one dies, that is just an illusion,' she interrupted. 'The body dies, the soul goes on always. In each lifetime we are just perfecting the soul, polishing the different facets of a jewel, till it is perfect.'

'Well,' I said, trying to stick to my point, 'someone who used to be here, but isn't any more . . .'

'Possession,' she said very slowly and clearly, 'is fifty per cent obsession. You hold on just as much as you are held on to. Only you can change. You must let go lovingly.' And the interview was over.

I went out and got into my car, my mind reeling. 'Possession is fifty per cent obsession.' It made perfect sense: because of all the guilt and the difficulty of our relationship, I had been holding on very tightly to Tate without realizing it. As I sat there I felt something shifting in my body – something very deep letting go. Suddenly I understood. Tate really had taken the earrings. It was her way of directing me to someone like Heddie. Someone who could warn me about my health, tell me the truth about myself, and teach me how to let go and set us both free. Tears poured down my face as I realized that taking the earrings was not an act of punishment, it was an act of love.

Nothing that Heddie said sounded strange to me. She just confirmed what I had known intuitively all along. I knew Tate hadn't died, she had simply changed form, moving from the visible to the invisible realm. Even what Heddie said about learning to see God in everything managed to slip past the radar of my rational mind and sink in – at least momentarily. There is so much more going on than we realize, I thought, in the big picture and in our own lives. We human beings are like mice in a cage busy measuring and formulating all sorts of laws and theories to define reality, without ever realizing that there are levels beyond our world, the knowledge of which blows our 'reality' to pieces.

Once we do see past the bars and realize that we are part of something so much bigger, then everything changes, I thought. The whole purpose of life changes. It becomes a question not of what can I do for myself, but how can I help? How can I live a life of truth and love and service? So what is it that I am meant to do? I wondered. Not knowing was so frustrating I wanted to march back into Heddie's house like a madwoman and shake her until she told me, but I restrained myself and drove home thinking about her advice. 'Rest and reflect,' she said. 'Take time. Realize what you are truly made of, then you will find your path.'

It was precisely the encouragement I needed to leave television. I wanted to leave London too, but I couldn't imagine where else in England I would live or what I would do once I got there. As Oregon had been such a haven to me in the past, it seemed the obvious place to go, and to my great relief my green card had come through just as I was finishing *Slice of Life*. So I decided to move to Bend, a small town 35 miles away from the Metolius, where my cousin Susie lived.

It sounds an easy choice, but it was an immensely difficult decision and I agonized over it, not least because it meant leaving my boyfriend Tom. We had been in a relationship for two years and although I had told him from the very beginning not to think long-term, because I was considering moving to America, he hadn't believed me. He hoped I would fall in love with him and decide to stay. He was right, I did fall in love with him, and his offer was so tempting. 'You don't need to go on making TV if you don't want to,' he assured me. 'But you don't have to go to America either. Stay here. I'll support you. You could have a baby, see friends, do all the things you enjoy.'

It would have been so easy to slip into the safety of his arms and the whole structure of marriage, instead of setting off into a completely unknown future on my own. 'Yes, yes,' urged my ego, wanting nothing more than a normal, comfortable life. 'Just give in. Get married, settle down, accept this is what life is like. It's what people do.' So easy. Except for the fact that my intuition was giving me a clear 'No!'

It seemed to me that by getting married I would be committing myself to a certain way of life, before I had found out what kind of life I wanted to live. It would be like locking myself into a cage, a golden cage perhaps, but a cage nonetheless. 'You're being ridiculous,' my ego argued, used to deciding what was best for my welfare and determined to stick to the old map of how my life was supposed to be. 'Marriage doesn't have to be like that. It's a wonderful thing: it provides love and security and a base in life. Besides, Tom's such a great person, of course it's the right thing to do.'

But no matter how much my ego advocated it, getting married didn't feel right, even though on a rational level I couldn't explain why. Because intuition comes from a much deeper place of knowing than the rational mind, it often isn't possible to understand its response in the moment. The 'why' only becomes clear later as life unfolds, which means that following one's intuition requires faith and surrender to the unknown. But I didn't know that then. All I knew was that things did not turn out well when I ignored my intuition – *Slice of Life* had been more than enough to teach me that. So I continued making plans to leave.

Most people I knew thought I was mad, and they were not at all reticent in telling me so.

'Your career is just taking off,' said my friend Edmund. 'You'd be crazy to stop now. Don't leave. Stay here and start your own production company instead.'

'What will you do over there, anyway?' asked Geoff.

Bonnie was the most adamant. 'You're throwing your life away!' she said.

My old boyfriend Ben was one of the few who encouraged me to go. 'What should I do?' I asked him over dinner one evening. 'Should I go to America or stay here, get married and live a nice, comfortable life?'

'Oh, for heaven's sake,' he said, 'don't get married. Go to America.'

'Are you jealous that I'm considering marrying some-one else?' I asked, wondering about the vehemence of his response.

'Don't flatter yourself,' he replied.

'Then what?'

'Because you have such a restless spirituality. You always have had, and you'll never be satisfied until you've found what you're looking for.'

'Oh,' I replied, genuinely taken aback.

Despite everything that Heddie had told me about polishing a facet of my soul, and despite the fact that I had spent the entire NLP training thinking about how to let in the light, it still hadn't sunk through my ego image of myself that I was on a spiritual journey. But I knew Ben was right. I was looking for something and it mattered to me more than marriage, more than fitting in, more than being safe. It helped me to know that I would make a misery of Tom's life too, if I married him against my instincts. So finally, still amidst tremendous anguish, I said goodbye to him, to my friends and family, my career, my home, even my cat and turned instead to that still, small voice inside.

I spent the first six weeks staying with Steve and Joan by the river. It was as beautiful as ever and as I hiked through the mountains I felt myself slowly coming back to life. But to my dismay the act of moving to America didn't provide any immediate answers. Instead I found myself standing on the frontier of my new life, alone, facing complete uncertainty. This is of course what life is actually like. We stand nose to nose with the unknown in every moment – we simply shield ourselves from this alarming truth with a constant supply of plans. For the first time in my life I didn't have any plans.

'It is a very confusing experience,' I wrote in my diary, 'giving up all I have known, for something I know nothing of. Sometimes I am elated and excited. Sometimes I am depressed and terrified. It is too hard, I think: there are too few clues. I am not strong enough to go through with this. But I am strong enough because I don't know what I would go back to. My whole spirit sinks at the thought of returning to London or England. So I'm strong enough only because I have no choice but to go on.'

I felt as if I had been stripped of everything. Like an actor divested of costume, make-up, role, script, I stood naked on an empty stage, once again wondering: Who am I? Without all the things I had used to define myself, I had absolutely no idea, and it felt like dying. In a sense 'I' was dying, because my old life, based on who I thought I was, had come to an end and my entire identity was shifting as I let go of my ego and came into alignment with my soul.

I was sitting on the deck one morning when I noticed a butterfly drifting through the columns of sunlight that filtered down through the pine trees. It settled on the table near my hand, copper wings slowly opening and closing. As I watched it I remembered reading about the stages of growth and transformation in the life cycle of a butterfly. In order for the butterfly to be born, the caterpillar has to die. In fact it dissolves into a pulp, in an extraordinary liquid meltdown of muscle and tissue from which the butterfly is then formed.

I guess that's what's happening to me, I thought: the old version of Catherine is melting down so that a new one can be born. 'Congratulations,' I said silently to the butterfly, feeling humbled. 'We are both destined to evolve and grow, butterflies and human beings alike, and you are way ahead of me. But if you can do it, I can.' I watched again as the butterfly turned slowly around on the table, wings still beating open and closed, simply being effortlessly itself. Perhaps that's it, I thought, perhaps that's the point, to be one's true self. Nothing more. Nothing less.

'It's about freeing myself from expectations,' I wrote in my diary. 'Money, career, even marriage: these have been drummed into me as the goals of life, and holding these expectations limits who I can be and what kind of life I can live. But they're society's values and not truly what my heart desires – at least they're not worth pursuing in their own right. So the more I separate from these beliefs the more it frees me to develop my identity and find the life that's right for me.

'It's also about making choices,' I realized, as I continued writing. 'And every choice matters, because in each moment we are creating our own future. In the bigger picture we are creating the world in which we live – the whole social and environmental catastrophe that we face is arising out of the individual, personal choices that we make. So it is vital to know: What do I really want? And who is the "I" that is choosing – my ego or my soul?'

In mid-September I moved in with Susie. She had a dear little yellow house, perched on the hillside overlooking the town of Bend, with a pretty garden and fantastic views of the sunrise. She was working night and day as an environmental activist, trying to protect the few remaining areas of old-growth forest in Oregon, and I soon got involved in her work. Three months flashed by in a blur of meetings, protests and demonstrations. We marched through the streets of Portland and camped outside in the forests, blockading roads so that logging trucks couldn't get through. I learnt about politics and environmental laws, civil disobedience and non-violent resistance. It was exciting and satisfying work and it allayed one of the fears I had about leaving television, which was that I wouldn't find anything else interesting to do.

It didn't earn me any money, however, which sent my inner bank manager into a riot of anxiety, and so doing it long term was not an option. Most importantly, when I checked in about it on a soul level, it didn't feel quite right, and I was endeavouring to let that be my guiding principle. If something felt right, I did it. If I had a sinking feeling about something, then I trusted that was not the direction for me to go in.

Using this new approach I swung around inside myself like a needle in a compass desperately trying to find the right course. I thought about contacting the local TV station. Sinking feeling. I had a proposal for a radio series. Sinking feeling. I was interested in multimedia and I had lots of ideas for CD-Roms. Sinking feeling. I realized that these ideas were all coming from my ego and what I already knew how to do, and I had the feeling that what I was being led towards was completely beyond anything I had ever known. Still, as one career option after another was ruled out, my ever-present doubts escalated. Was I crazy? Should I have left England? Should I have got married? What was I going to do about money?

On top of all these doubts, I was lonely. Much as I loved spending time with Susie, I missed Tom and my friends. I missed dinner parties and weekends away. I missed going to art galleries and the theatre. Bend was a sweet little town, with a couple of cafés and a decent bookshop, but it didn't offer much in the form of culture or entertainment. 'Let's go out tonight,' I suggested to Susie one Saturday morning, as I flicked through the local paper, the *Bend Bulletin*. 'There's a band playing in one of the bars downtown.'

'OK,' she said, 'but don't get your hopes up.'

It was too late, I already had.

The band was beyond awful and I stood at the bar in a state of shock, wearing a black satin mini-skirt printed with red roses and a plain black shirt, which I had bought in Paris. My thoughts drifted to the weekend I had spent there with Tom, visiting museums by day and the most stylish clubs by night.

'Wanna beer?' a man asked me, jolting me back into real time. I looked up. He was wearing a cowboy hat. I looked down. Yup, boots and spurs.

'Er, no, thank you,' I replied, and in that moment I began to really get the enormity of the change I had made in my life.

'What on earth am I doing?' I asked Susie, for the five-hundredth time, as we drove home. 'Am I making a terrible mistake?'

Wisely she remained silent, which allowed me to hear once more the unwavering reply of my soul. 'No.'

14. From Ego to Soul

At Christmas I went to stay with my father in California. He, Vicki and Valentine had moved to America in 1990 and settled near a small town just north of San Diego, where they opened a restaurant. Their house was large and comfortable, built in the classic southern California open-plan style, with high vaulted ceilings and lots of light. There were avocado and lemon trees in the garden, and a swimming pool, which my father had surrounded with a profusion of vibrantly coloured and deliciously fragrant flowering plants.

After the New Year, as I got ready to go back to Oregon, Vicki encouraged me to stay. 'We would love to have you with us,' she said. 'You're welcome to be here for as long as you want.' I checked into what felt right. Oregon? Sinking feeling. Stay here? Neutral. Go somewhere else? Neutral. So I stayed. It was certainly an easy place to be and I felt tremendously lucky to have the time to spend with my family. It allowed me to get to know Dad in a new way – not as a child, but as a grown-up. I became much closer to Vicki, and I enjoyed being with Valentine, who at ten years old was an incredibly bright little boy, fascinated by life and all its mysteries.

That much was good. The rest of my life was rather more challenging. Despite feeling I had made the right decision in leaving London, I was still confused and frightened. My future loomed before me, empty and enormous, and I had no plan. 'It will be OK,' my soul reassured me. 'You have relied on your ego and your rational mind to guide you for your entire life: now you are switching to a different way of being, and that is hard. Very hard. It takes time and patience and perseverance and you are doing it. You have already made huge changes. Just keep going. Let yourself want what you really want – not just what your ego wants – and this will help you discover who you truly are.'

But what do I want? I wondered. It was sobering to realize that I had become so disconnected from the real me that I didn't know what I wanted. Although, as I thought about my decision to leave England, I realized that actually I did know: it was just very difficult to act upon it. In my lifetime pursuit of trying to fit in and get love, I had learnt to override and deny what felt right and what I wanted to such an extent that I no longer recognized my feeling of 'no' as my own. Or I judged it and made myself wrong. Wrong for not wanting to go on working in television. Wrong for not wanting to get married.

I was starting to see that my inner voice, the voice of my soul, was actually the voice of my true 'yes' and 'no'. And that by coming into alignment with my soul, I was coming into alignment with the real me, because my soul and I were not separate. Clearly my soul had a far greater knowledge and wisdom than I did on the personality level. It had a vision and long-range plan beyond my ability to see, and yet we were one and the same. And so by following my soul, I was healing the split I had lived with all my life between who I thought I ought to be and who I actually was.

And that was simultaneously wonderful and terrifying.

It is wonderful to know that one will get fit by exercising. Or to know that one will learn to play the piano by practising. It is another thing entirely to actually do it. In this case shifting my way of operating and my identity from my ego to my soul meant letting go of what I thought my life should look like and who I thought I was. It meant letting go of control and the idea that I knew what was best for me. It meant surrender, not just once, but continuously. I had never done anything so terrifying.

My ego was not willing to give up without a fight. 'This is madness,' it said. 'Bonnie was right: you are throwing your life away. What is the matter with you – why can't you see what a terrible mistake you are making? You have walked away from everything – and now what? What are you going to do next? You don't have the faintest idea, do you? Sweetheart,' it said, oh so convincingly, 'listen to me: we need a plan. Let's go back to England. Or at least get a job here. There is so much we can achieve. We can't just sit back and do nothing for the rest of our life . . .'

As my ego went on and on, desperately trying to retain control, my doubts proliferated exponentially, running in an endless loop through my mind. I barely had time to open my eyes in the morning before they started up again: Am I making a terrible mistake? Should I have left England? Should I have got married? If I went back now would Tom still marry me? Am I ever going to be normal? How am I going to earn money? Should I have given up television? Will I ever be happy? Is it too late to change my mind? Why am I doing this to myself? And what the hell is it that I am doing anyway?

To which my soul, ever steadfast, replied: 'You are becoming your true Self.'

I just have to have faith, I kept telling myself. Faith in my intuition. Faith in myself. Faith in the unfolding of life itself. And I remembered an exercise from the NLP training called 'Act As If'. So I did, and in the process I discovered that you don't proceed on faith because you have enough faith already. You proceed because you have to and along the way you create the faith you need.

Unable to answer any of the long-term questions of my life, like what I really wanted or what my purpose was, I turned to more immediate concerns. I was still physically exhausted from *Slice of Life* and all the years of stress and overwork prior to that. I knew that if I was ever going to accomplish anything I had to let my body heal. So in the New Year I did a cleansing fast for a week and then resumed my regular diet. Over the years I had discovered that certain things, especially sugar, wheat and alcohol, drastically affected my mental clarity and my energy levels, so I made a point of not eating them, concentrating instead on vegetables, protein and very little carbohydrate. After the cleanse my clarity returned: I felt clearer and lighter, my mind sharpened, but the problem of low energy seemed deeper than that.

One morning I went out to my car and discovered that the battery was flat. I borrowed my father's car and took the battery to a local garage to have it recharged. The mechanic hooked it up to a machine and shook his head. 'It's dead,' he said. 'I can't recharge it. You'll have to buy another.' I drove home wondering if I had inadvertently done the same thing to my own body.

'What can I do?' I asked my body.

'Yoga,' it replied.

'Fine,' I hastily agreed, and started looking for a teacher. I discovered that Tim Miller, one of the world's top astanga yoga teachers, lived and taught about half an hour away from my father's house, in a little seaside town called Encinitas. Excitedly I told Vicki about him. 'Yes,' she said, 'I know. I went to a class with him once. The studio was full of people doing incredible contortions. He seemed nice, though, and offered to teach me, but I was so intimidated I didn't dare go back.'

I thought she must be exaggerating, so I set off anyway, but it was exactly as she had described. There were about twenty men and women, who were all tanned, extremely fit and unbelievably flexible, bending their bodies into positions that seemed impossible. The walls of the studio were painted green with purple lotus flowers and there was an altar at the front decorated with statues of various Indian deities. I hesitated for a moment in the doorway, feeling like a very ungainly mortal who had somehow stumbled into the training room of the gods. Then I slunk into one of the corners, unrolled my yoga mat and hoped no one would notice that I couldn't touch my toes.

There was, however, no escaping Tim's vigilant eye. Tall, with shoulder-length curly brown hair and a body worthy of Shiva, he came over and introduced himself.

'Have you done yoga before?' he asked.

'Um, not really,' I answered, wishing that I could shrivel up on the spot. 'I know some of the basic poses, but that's it.'

'Well,' he replied, 'this may be a little different from the classes you have done before. I teach astanga yoga, which means that we work through a particular sequence of poses. Here is a sheet for you to follow until you can remember the order. And unlike other classes where everybody does the same thing at once, here people work at their own pace while I teach and adjust each person individually. Do you know how to do Surya Namaskar A?'

I looked at him blankly.

'The sun salutation?'

I nodded.

'Great, that's the first pose,' he said, and pointed at the sheet. 'Do five of those and I'll be back to help you.'

So I began, and it was agony. Tim came back several times, patiently adjusting my body and showing me the correct alignment for each pose.

'Tight hamstrings!' he said, as he positioned me into downward-facing dog. 'Much pain?'

'Much pain,' I groaned, still upside down.

'It's only sensation,' he commented. 'Just witness it and keep breathing,' and he moved on to adjust my neighbour.

Hard as it was, the physical pain paled in comparison to the mental anguish I inflicted on myself about not being able to do the poses properly. 'Keep your eyes on your mat,' Tim told me several times, but I couldn't. I kept looking around the room, comparing myself with everyone else and always coming back to the basic point that I was worthless because other people were better at yoga than me.

'Yoga is about self-acceptance,' Tim said, as he stretched me into a spinal twist. 'It is not about comparing or judging or wanting to do better. It is about loving yourself right now, just as you are.'

Oh really, I thought, not knowing that this would turn

out to be one of the most important lessons yoga had to teach me.

At the end of class I limped back to my car, feeling as if I had been wrung through a mangle physically and psychologically.

'Happy now?' I asked my body, a trifle sarcastically.

'Oh yes,' it replied.

'Seriously?'

'Yes.'

'You mean we have to go back?'

'Definitely. Every day.'

'Every day???'

'Yes.'

I went back the next day and the next and pretty much every day for the next six months. Most of the poses on the sheet that Tim had given me to follow were completely beyond me and my perfectionist went into overdrive. The classes were held in silence, but the noise level in my head was deafening as my inner critic ranted and raved.

'I'm so stiff and tight,' I said to Tim after one particularly difficult class. 'I'm never going to be good at this.'

'The practice of the yoga poses teaches us to pay attention and to be present right now with whatever is happening, without judging it or ourselves,' he answered. 'So being good at yoga has nothing to do with how flexible you are, it is about how kind and loving you can be towards yourself. Everybody's body is different. Some people are naturally more supple and therefore it's easier for them to do the poses. This does not make them better yogis or better people. So there is nothing but suffering to be gained from comparison.'

After weeks of listening to him, the truth of his words

finally started to sink in. My perfectionism had met its match. I could not will or force myself to be better at yoga, and I had to face the fact that I would probably never be good at it on the level of physical performance. But, amazingly, it was dawning on me that it didn't matter. I could see how ridiculous it was to believe that my value depended on how well I could do something, be it yoga poses or anything else. It's just the same old story, I realized – that I have to be perfect in order to be lovable – and it is simply not true. So I let it go.

The peace that followed was extraordinary. My mind was quiet and there was no harping voice berating me for not being good enough. In the quiet I started paying attention to what was going on in my body. Everything hurt. So much so that one day it struck me that I didn't actually want to be in my body because it was too painful, and I had a flashback to a conversation I'd had with Frances, when we both lived at my flat in London. 'Sometimes I think I am only in this much of my body,' I said to her, and I brought my hand to the bridge of my nose, indicating that I lived only in the top three inches of my head. Now I realized just how true that statement was.

But working through the poses every day helped to gradually release the physical pain and tension and it also brought about emotional catharsis – I often burst into tears as waves of grief and sadness moved through my body. Sometimes the feelings were so intense that I lay on my mat sobbing, while the rest of the class proceeded around me. Tim didn't bat an eye. 'Good, good,' he said, as he wandered by, 'cry as much as you need to.'

Over time, as my body literally became habitable, I could feel myself dropping deeper and deeper inside it. I felt like I was finally arriving, choosing at last to be here in my body, on the earth. I remembered something Robert had told me: 'The point of healing is not just to become physically healthy, important though that is. The point is to incarnate and become whole in mind, body and spirit, so that we can be fully here and fully alive.' I was beginning to understand what he meant.

I soon learnt to tell the difference between the stiffness caused by a lifetime's lack of stretching and the more chronic areas of tension in my body, and I noticed that one of my biggest problem areas was in my sacrum. I felt as if I had a block there and it became clear that my lack of energy was directly related to it. It was like hitting a wall, because when I used up what little energy I did have each day, I came face to face with the block. At that point, generally no more than halfway through class, I would collapse on to my mat, exhausted.

A month passed and I felt more and more frustrated. One day, I realized I couldn't fight it. Instead I tried tuning in, hoping to find out what the block was. I lay quietly, emptied my mind and let my awareness feel into it. The image that came to me was of tundra – something frozen solid, ancient, impenetrable, lifeless. I was mystified. What was I doing with tundra in my body? But I began to work with the image, using the yoga poses and the thawing power of my breath to help release it. Over the next few weeks the block slowly transformed from tundra into granite. It wasn't exactly what I had hoped for, but it was definitely a change, and that was encouraging.

When I was not doing yoga, I went on trying to figure out what to do with the rest of my life. 'You owe it to your higher self to do what you came to this earth to do.' Heddie's words often echoed through my mind, but I didn't feel as if I were any closer to finding out what that meant. If only I knew what my purpose was, I thought, then it would be easy, because I could skip all this horrible waiting and not knowing and just get on with it.

But, frustrating as it was in the beginning, I have come to see that living in the unknown is actually a wonderful place to be. For the place of not knowing is the place of infinite potential. The place where the creative force of the universe unfolds. The trouble is that most of the time, because we are so frightened of the unknown, we try to control and plan our whole lives, and end up disconnected from the flow of life. But when we dwell in the unknown we have the chance to let life live itself through us. Which means we are open to the creative force – the power of Divine Love manifesting itself through the physical world. And that is what life truly is: the movement of Love.

However, living that way involves surrender and trust, and that is a hard thing to learn.

'So what am I supposed to do now?' I asked my soul. 'Surely I've got to do something?'

'Be patient and the next step will become clear,' my soul replied. 'You are still discovering who you truly are. Only when you know that will you discover what your purpose is and how you can best be of service. So you must keep listening and trust that things will reveal themselves bit by bit.'

And that was so difficult, especially when the process it was taking all my strength and courage to go through didn't look like anything from the outside.

'But what am I supposed to say to people when they ask what I do?' I asked, somewhat petulantly.

'Say you do nothing,' my soul said.

'I can't say that,' I protested. 'People will think I am mad, lazy, selfish, a nobody, a good-for-nothing . . .'

'You have to remember that your identity and value is not dependent on what you do: that is one of the lessons you need to learn,' replied my soul. 'And anyway, those are your own judgements. The truth is you don't know what people will think and it doesn't matter. That is another important lesson for you – it doesn't matter what other people think.'

Not long after this a friend called Frederick, who I had met through yoga, invited me to a party. He lived in an amazing house right on the beach in Encinitas. It had curved adobe walls that blended in beautifully with the sandy cliffs and a large coastal desert garden with meandering pebble paths and lots of different cacti, succulents and sage, interspersed with large and beautiful sculptures.

When I arrived at about 9 p.m. there were lots of people dancing outside on the patio to a live band. The night was warm and the garden was lit by candles and torches and stars blazing from a deep-blue sky. It had been ten months since I had been to a party and I was in heaven. When the band finished I wandered into the house and bumped into a group of people from yoga. As I was chatting with them, a man I didn't know joined us and we ended up talking to each other.

'I'm called Joel,' he said after a few minutes.

'My name's Catherine,' I replied.

'And what do you do, Catherine?' he asked.

I stood there like a goldfish, my mouth opening and

closing, as I tried to decide what to say. Eventually I squeezed out the word, 'Nothing.' My voice was very tight and small.

'Oh,' he said, looking interested. 'What kind of nothing?'

'I honestly don't know. I'm learning to listen to my soul and let it guide me through life, and at this point it's all completely unknown. My old life has come to an end and the form of my new life hasn't emerged yet. So I'm just trusting that something will happen.' I stopped, unable to believe I was actually saying this out loud, let alone to someone I had never met before.

'I see,' he nodded. 'So you're going through a metamorphosis – like a butterfly. Scary, isn't it?'

'Yes – I spend half my time wondering if I'm crazy.'

'You're definitely not crazy. Letting go of all you have known and everything that seems safe in order to follow your soul is a hard thing to do. But it is also brave and beautiful. When we learn how to live in alignment with our soul, we give the world a great gift, because we let the light of God shine through us. So don't be frightened. Just trust the process.'

I wasn't sure what to say in reply to this, and I was grateful when another person from yoga came over to talk to us. The conversation changed and after a few minutes I excused myself and went back outside. Later, as I was leaving, I walked past Joel and said goodbye. 'Goodbye, butterfly woman,' he replied, handing me his card. 'Call me if you want someone to talk to.' The following morning I noticed it lying upside down on the table where I had put my keys and purse. There was a quote printed on the back of it: 'Of your ego you can do nothing to save yourself or others, but of your spirit you can do everything for the salvation of both. *A Course in Miracles.*' I stood there for a moment looking at it, my heart pounding. Then I picked the card up and put it in between the pages of my diary. I didn't ever see Joel again – I was too scared to call him.

15. Love and Only Love

When I woke in the morning there was often thick fog pressed against the window, blocking the view. My bedroom was on the ground floor and the window looked out over a flowerbed, across a wide driveway and up a steep bank planted with shrubs and trees. If I didn't know there was a whole world out there, I mused to myself one day as I got dressed, I would think this dense white wall of nothingness was all there was. A few mornings later, as I lay in bed immobilized by the usual stampede of doubt and fear, it dawned on me that just as the fog blanked out the rest of the world, my thoughts were obscuring my vision and blocking me from seeing the truth and the bigger picture of what was happening to me.

En masse the doubts seemed so convincing and real that they were all I could see. Yet when I examined them one by one, they were patently not true. It is all a matter of what I listen to, I realized. Do I listen to the voice of doubt or to the voice of my intuition? Ego or soul? But what a battle it was. All I can do, I thought, as I forced myself to get out of bed and drive to yoga, is keep having faith. And trust that eventually my doubts will dissipate in the light of the truth, just as the fog evaporates in the morning sun.

I knew that until that happened I was not in a fit state of mind to make any decisions. So I steadied myself and did my best to witness the clamour of my mind without acting on it. It was like watching a one-woman show in which I played all the different parts. First of all there was me – desperately trying to figure out what the hell was going on. Then there was my soul – urging me onwards towards truth and wholeness. There was my ego – the part of me that was concerned with survival, seeking comfort, and winning love and approval. And in cahoots with this was my inner critic, which I would learn is called the superego in psychology. But as I didn't know that then, I began calling it by the name that seemed most appropriate: the tyrant.

I realized this part of me had developed as a protection mechanism. As children we internalize the voices of our parents and those who have authority over us in an attempt to avoid their criticism by criticizing ourselves first. So the superego becomes an internal judge, monitoring our performance and policing what we are and aren't allowed to do. The trouble is that over time it becomes so judgemental and critical that it ends up causing immense suffering, as well as severely limiting what we allow ourselves to do.

As I listened to my internal dialogue – 'You're making a big mistake. You're doing this all wrong. You're never going to achieve anything ever again.' – I realized how much of it was coming from my inner critic. Unfortunately, I discovered that, unlike removing outdated software from a computer, I couldn't just switch it off or delete it from my mind. Instead I had to learn not to fall for its stories, just as I had to learn not to buy into my doubts.

So again, the first challenge was to recognize when my doubts and inner critic were running riot, which was very difficult, given how habitual and familiar they were. So it was often only when I was really hurting that I thought: Wait a minute, what is going on here? Then I had to work out how to deal with them. I started by trying to reason with them and explain why I was choosing to do things differently from now on. But that proved to be futile, because nothing I said made any difference. So then I simply started to say, 'No, that is not the truth.' Which was very effective for a short time, by which I mean however long it took me to get sucked back in.

The whole process was utterly brutal and I often felt like I was being beaten to pieces by my fear and self-doubt. There were many times when I wanted to give up and run away. But there was nowhere to run away to, because the only way out was through. So I kept on paying attention and the more I learnt to witness my thoughts and name them – 'This is self-doubt' or 'This is self-criticism' – without getting caught up in them, the more I saw they were simply habits of my mind and not the truth. So gradually, step by tiny step, the power they held over me lessened and my trust in my intuition and the voice of my soul grew stronger. And the more I trusted my soul the easier things became and the more I felt at peace.

Soon it was the beginning of April, and although I had been going to yoga every day for three months, much to my annoyance the block was still there. From tundra it had slowly changed to granite and from granite to sandstone. I recalled the sandstone I had seen and loved so much on a trip to Utah – great sun-warmed chunks of it that were gently eroded by wind and time into the finest, silkiest dust that simply blew away – and I felt sure success was at hand. Still, I was intrigued. Where had the block come from? I used the technique Clare had taught me of tracking the feeling back through time to find out where it had originated in my life. It was easy to follow, but it didn't seem to stop anywhere, as if it had begun before my life had, and I began to have the strange feeling that the block didn't actually belong to me, even though it was having such a profound effect.

I came home from class one day so tired that I crawled back into bed, where I had the idea to talk to the block. 'Block,' I said, 'I want to thank you for being here, because I am sure you have something important to teach me. So will you please tell me what you are and where you came from?' A shadow flickered in the back of my mind, like a thick, black curtain being pulled aside and Granny, my maternal grandmother, appeared.

She died when I was twelve and I remembered her as a dour, bitter, grey-haired old woman, who frightened me. She lived on the other side of the island and Tate used to visit her once a week and take her grocery shopping. Sometimes I went too, but I don't recall ever staying overnight, or playing with her, or even having a conversation. After her death I didn't think to ask about her, and so I was quite unprepared for what she had to say.

'I felt so much creativity and excitement about life when I was a young woman,' she told me. 'Then I got married. I didn't really want to, I didn't feel like I had found the right man. But your grandfather wanted to marry me, and it was expected. So I agreed. The whole thing was very frustrating. I had no outlet for the joy and creativity I felt, and after a while I simply closed those parts of me down. It was too painful living with them – they were a constant reminder of a life I couldn't lead. So I shut them down and they settled inside me like a stone.'

So was this my stone. On one level it seemed impossible, and yet it made a certain kind of sense. I wondered if Tate had carried it too. And did Bonnie? Had it been passed down through the blood from mother to daughter? Clearly we inherit a lot more than our physical characteristics, I realized. Big noses and a susceptibility to certain diseases are just the beginning. There is a whole package of stuff – physical and psychological.

Granny's story convinced me more than ever that if we cannot resolve our experiences as they are happening, our body has no choice but to store them until such time as we can. If we don't ever get around to healing and releasing them, then eventually they manifest as illness and dysfunction. And that gets passed on to the next generation. Which makes it even more important that we attempt to heal ourselves.

Why don't we know about this sort of thing? I wondered, although I would soon learn that there are plenty of people who do. The great psychologist Carl Jung believed that some of our complexes are more than a hundred years old. And in the yoga tradition the process of accumulating experiences in the body is well understood. Despite months of practice my hamstrings were still as taut as steel cables.

'Why am I so tight?' I asked Tim, as he released me from some contortion designed to stretch these offending ligaments.

'*Samskaras*,' he replied.

'What?'

'*Samskaras* are tendencies, habits, memories held in the body. Sometimes they are generated in this lifetime. Sometimes they are passed down through the generations. Part of the purpose of yoga is to free ourselves of *avidya* – the unconsciousness caused by the build-up of such patterns.'

Oh, I thought to myself, as Tim walked away, I guess that's what I have been learning to do all my life, to free myself from *avidya* – I just didn't know it had a name. Then I thought: How amazing – these yoga guys have obviously been aware of this for thousands of years, and for the first time it dawned on me that a spiritual path might have some real wisdom to offer.

Wonderful as the yoga was, I still found my greatest joy and inspiration in nature. My father's house was in a typical southern Californian suburban area and for true wilderness one had to drive a couple of hours inland to the stark, awe-inspiring silence of the Anza-Borrego Desert or to the Cuyamaca Mountains. I had a new friend called Loni, who shared my passion for hiking, and we set off to the Cuyamacas whenever possible.

Although they were called mountains, they were actually rolling hills, scattered with groves of Californian live oaks and ponderosa pines. On one gorgeous sunny day in May we followed a trail that wound up through the trees. As it had so many times before, my heart started singing the moment we began to walk and within a few minutes I was filled with the pure, unquenchable joy of being alive. After a couple of miles the trail led out into a wide open meadow filled with wild flowers. Loni knew all their names and pointed them out to me – footsteps-of-spring, wild peonies,

Indian paintbrush, lupins and cream-cups. Meadow larks filled the air with a cascade of liquid song, hawks and vultures soared above, and we both staggered around like a pair of drunks, intoxicated by the beauty of it all.

We hiked on for a few more miles and passed through a grove of oak trees. The air was warm and fragrant, sunlight dappled through the trees, squirrels busied themselves on the ground searching for acorns, and woodpeckers swooped to and fro above. The place was rich with effortless activity, each creature abiding by its own nature with the utmost simplicity. I had the feeling that if you could enter into a state of complete clarity this is what it would be like. And I wanted that – wanted to live my own life from that pure simplicity of being.

By the time we reached our car it was late afternoon and we were tired and happy after a ten-mile hike. I got home to find that Vicki had left a note on my bed. It was a page pulled from her *Little Zen* calendar. The quote for that day read: 'The mountains, rivers, earth, grasses, trees and forests are always emanating a subtle precious light, day and night, always emanating a subtle precious sound, demonstrating and expounding to all people the unsurpassed ultimate truth. Yuan-sou.' Exactly so, I thought. Exactly so.

I went upstairs to thank her. She and Valentine were leaving for Hawaii the next day and she was sitting on the floor of her room packing.

'Did you get my note?' she asked, smiling. 'I thought it was perfect for you.'

'Yes, it's so true – there is this subtle light. I experienced it today in the woods. I don't know what it is, but I know it's there.'

'I'm sure you will understand in time,' she said, standing up to give me a hug. 'Now, you will be all right without us?'

'Yes, of course, although I'll miss you.'

'And you will look after your father?'

'Absolutely.'

Every May Vicki, Valentine and Vicki's sister Coralee went to Hawaii for two weeks. Dad insisted on staying behind to look after the business, which meant that he and I were on our own. In the mornings I went to yoga while he went to the restaurant to do the books, and we met back at the house to have lunch together. We sat outside by the pool, in the shade of the veranda, and ate tomato salad, with avocados picked from the garden and home-grown basil, which Dad derived great amusement from pronouncing American style: bay-zel! Exclamation mark included.

'It's not a bad place to be, is it?' he would ask, looking around at the flowers and the hummingbirds and the endlessly blue sky.

'No, Dad, it's not a bad place to be at all,' I'd reply.

So our conversation began most days. We shared memories, talked about books, about his life and Tate's. It was fascinating to hear about his childhood and life as a young man, with all the dreams he'd had and the choices he'd made. It was like filling a black-and-white photograph with colour, bringing alive this person I had known all my life and yet felt as if I barely knew at all.

One afternoon Dad was upstairs filing paperwork, one of his least-favourite activities, and I took him a cup of tea. He waved his hand at the piles of paper surrounding him. 'I just don't know what to do with it all,' he said, clearly exasperated. 'And there's something else I don't know what to do with either – all the family photo albums.'

'What family?' I asked, not really getting it.

'Our family,' he replied and beckoned me to his wardrobe, where he pulled one of at least a dozen albums off a shelf. I sat on the floor and flipped hungrily from page to page.

Here were Dad and Tate on honeymoon in Corsica – Tate posing in a bikini, looking so fresh and young and pretty. Bonnie as a little girl. Geoff as a baby. Me as a baby. Puppies and chicks and guinea pigs. Fishing boats, oyster beds and mud. Granny and Gramp, wearing Christmas-cracker hats, looking like cartoon grandparents they were so old and wrinkled and scary. Ponies and horses of all shapes and sizes. Holidays in Brittany, Ireland and Scotland. Dodpits' renovation under way: doors moved, walls built, the garden planted. School photos and dreadful uniforms. Christmas trees all decorated and glittering and surrounded by piles of presents. Parties and flowery dresses that I can still remember to this day . . .

They were happy photos. Suddenly I could appreciate what a marvellous thing Dad and Tate had given us, with the life and house they built together. And how much effort had gone into it all and how hard they had tried to take care of us. Often my eyes were so blurred with tears I could hardly see – but there it was right in front of me: we were happy after all, the photos proved it. 'But it doesn't add up,' I wrote in my diary later that day. 'The searing pain of feeling unloved and the terror of being abandoned is so strong and real, that here I am, thirty-one years old and still trying to heal myself from its impact. I just don't understand.'

A few days later I plucked up the courage to ask Dad about it at lunch.

'Dad,' I said, 'I know you love me now, but did you love me when I was little?'

'Yes, of course I did,' he said, absolutely astonished, a forkful of tomato salad suspended in mid-air. 'Very much.'

'Did Tate?'

'Yes!'

'Then how come I didn't know that growing up?' I asked.

'You were such a pet,' my father said, shaking his head sadly, 'everyone adored you. How could you possibly not have known that you were loved?'

'Because everyone was so angry all the time and I was scared that Tate was going to abandon me and you were always away and I never felt good enough to deserve your love anyway and . . .' I stopped as I saw the look of pain and dismay on Dad's face.

'I do regret,' he said, after a moment's pause, 'that I was so busy working. I feel that in many ways I missed your childhood, but I was also doing my best to build a business and support us all.'

'I know, Dad – I'm not blaming, really. I can see from the photos how hard you and Tate both worked to create a wonderful home for us, and I appreciate that so much. I appreciate all the things you did for me. But it wasn't easy, was it?'

'No,' he replied. 'It wasn't easy.'

Still confused I went back and looked at the photos again, sitting as before on the floor of Dad's wardrobe. I paid special attention to Tate, and there they were, in so many of the pictures: the tell-tale signs – her eyebrows, arched and menacing, and her eyes that burned with a dark, smouldering fire. Hers was not the face of a happy woman. Oh poor Tate, I thought, feeling a surge of compassion and understanding. Poor Dad.

For years I had thought my parents were screwed up because they had problems. Now I could see they were screwed up because they had problems and no skills to deal with them in a conscious way. They didn't know how to take responsibility for what was happening and change it. They couldn't talk openly and honestly to each other about how they felt. They couldn't see that the hurts and wounds of their pasts were replaying in the present, or see how to use each other as mirrors showing them where they needed to heal. Most importantly, they didn't know that if they addressed their problems, the very things that were causing so much pain and conflict would bring them closer – closer to themselves, closer to each other, closer to love.

And yet there they were, bound together by marriage and trying to raise a family. I began to see the complexity of it all. Of course there was love, but not only had it often seemed so conditional; it had also been buried so much of the time under the tension and fighting, that as a little girl it was invisible to me.

There were no bells or flashing lights accompanying this realization. Just a quiet feeling of relief and ease spreading through my body. I lay on the floor of the wardrobe, my eyes scanning across Dad's clothes – shirts mostly pale blue, sweaters mostly dark blue or grey, tastefully spotted and striped ties that he no longer wore, and smart black lace-up shoes that had also been abandoned in favour of the casual California style and comfort of sneakers. And as I lay there, I could feel things reorganizing themselves inside and clicking into place as the truth sank in: my family had loved me all along.

That night Dad and I had dinner together.

'You know what I said the other day at lunch about not feeling loved?' I asked him.

'Yes.'

'Well, I just wanted you to know that I figured it out. I realize now that of course you loved me, and I didn't want you to worry about it.'

'Good,' he said. 'I was worried. You're right: things weren't easy between your mother and me, but that wasn't your fault, and I'm sorry for the hurt it caused you.'

After that we watched a video and the next morning I got up and went to yoga. Since my conversation with Granny the block had completely vanished. My energy levels had improved dramatically and I was starting to enjoy doing yoga. I was getting fitter and more flexible – now even I could touch my toes. I also felt more solid, more alive, more at home in my body than I had ever felt before.

At the end of class I was lying in savassana, the final relaxation pose. The room was quiet and my mind was still. An image came to me. I saw Tate as a spirit, soaring and floating like an incredibly beautiful kite, and I was flooded with the feeling of unconditional love. All the hurt and disappointment I carried inside melted away and in that moment I realized that love is not only infinite, it is all there is. When we experience hurt and anger and grief, those feelings are real to us, but at a deeper level they are simply misunderstandings, just as it would be a misunderstanding to think that the sun no longer existed simply because a cloud blocked it from view. Tate was joined by Granny and the two of them soared together.

'Thank you,' Granny said, the words forming in my mind. 'Thank you for breaking the patterns. The work you're doing is helping all of us.'

A few moments later they disappeared and I lay on the floor, my whole being awash with love.

As I drove home from class, I noticed that something in me was singing: 'This is the way . . . This is the way . . . This is the way to freedom.' Over and over again the phrase repeated. I reflected on the different stages of healing I had been through in my life — physically, emotionally, psychologically and now at last spiritually — and realized that they were different aspects of the same process. I am becoming whole, I thought, with a sudden start of amazement. I am becoming who I really am! 'This is the way . . . This is the way . . . This is the way to freedom!'

16. Coming Home

At the end of June I went back to England. When I left the previous summer I had promised myself that I would stay in America for a year and then go back to reconsider my decision. 'You must be looking forward to seeing everyone,' Vicki said, as she and Dad drove me to the airport.

'Yes,' I replied, my stomach churning with a mixture of excitement and dread.

'Please send them all our love.'

'Of course.'

'It will be a test,' Dad suggested, 'a way to find out where you really want to be.'

I nodded. On a soul level I felt the decision had already been made, and I was pretty sure I would return. But my ego was still clinging to the hope that once I got back to England I would snap out of this 'crazy thinking' and return to a 'normal' life.

My friend Amanda met me at Heathrow Airport.

'I've missed you so much,' she said, giving me a big hug.

'I've missed you too,' I replied, my eyes filling with tears at the pleasure of seeing her again. We drove into London, dropped off my bags at her flat and went straight out to lunch to celebrate. After the wide-open horizons of California it was shocking to find myself back in the city, and I looked out of her car in a daze, at streets so familiar and now so strange.

'Does it feel funny to be back?' she asked.

'Very,' I answered.

From London I went to stay with Bonnie, from Bonnie to Geoff, from Geoff to my aunt La and back to London again. I visited all my friends and took my place as godmother at the christening of Frances' first baby. It was lovely to see everyone, and wherever I went people told me how well and happy I looked. It was true. I did look well – tanned, fit and relaxed. Compared to how I had been when I left England the summer before the transformation seemed miraculous, and as I walked around London I felt it more fully than ever. Felt it in my bones and my muscles, the power of a new life and vitality surging through me.

I was greeted not only with love and affection, but also with the inevitable questions. Everybody wanted to know what I had been doing and what I was going to do next. Questions I did not have the answers to. I felt guilty about not working, and the words 'yoga' and 'hiking' choked in my throat. Talking about my inner journey was even harder and I felt awkward and embarrassed even mentioning it. At that point I dearly wished I had some role model, someone to whom I could refer and say, Look, I am doing what they have done. Or an established path that I could follow, leading to a specified – and successful – destination. But in my world those things did not exist and as a result the kind of inner work I had been doing was not widely understood or respected. I didn't fully understand or respect it myself, so how could I expect anyone else to?

I had been in England for about a month when my ex-boyfriend Tom suggested I could stay at his mother's cottage in Herefordshire for a few days if I wanted some time on my own. I leapt at the chance. This little stone cottage, tucked into the end of a valley, with a garden of herbs and roses, surrounded by fields of sheep and woods that rose steeply up to a broad open ridge, was one of my favourite places in England. Tom even lent me his car and I set off westwards down the motorway, singing my heart out to one of the tapes I found on the back seat, by a band called Odyssey. It was early Seventies soul, rich, earthy, fabulous: 'I'm going back to my roots, yeah!' As if I had any idea what that actually meant or how close I was to finding out.

I arrived at the cottage in the late afternoon, parked, and immediately set off up the ridge. Wave after wave of hills spread out around me. Sunlight flooded the slopes, glinting from outcrops of rock and pooling in the golden fields of corn. Trees and wind danced. The rhythmic bleating of sheep and the liquid, cascading song of a skylark mingled in the air with my own cries of delight.

For the first time since I had been back in England I felt my spirit soar with joy, arcing across earth and sky from one horizon to the next, meeting the land and the life that was being lived all around me. All the doubts, all the questions and uncertainty dropped away. 'This is what I want!' I shouted out to the startled sheep. 'I want to live with this feeling of connection every day!' And I resolved again to do whatever it would take to create that.

Slowly I floated down through the woods, into the gathering twilight, and settled into the cottage. I made vegetable soup, which I ate at the old pine table in the kitchen with almost as much relish as I consumed the peace and quiet. Despite the fact I had spent a lot of time in America on my own, I had never been completely alone there, certainly not for a whole twenty-four hours or more. With a deep sigh of relief, I sank into the velvety embrace of silence and solitude.

I slept that night in the upstairs room of the converted barn next to the cottage. It felt holy to me, clean and spartan like a chapel or a monk's cell. The roughly hewn stone walls were soft, powdery white. Wooden beams reached up above me, meeting at the tips like hands in prayer. A huge window spanned from floor to ceiling, looking out over the garden and the dark shadows cast by a magnificent old walnut tree. I curled up in bed and drifted off to sleep listening to the murmur of the wind and the distant drone of the sheep.

I spent the next couple of days walking and lying under the fresh green peppery-scented leaves of the walnut tree, writing in my diary and reading. Then on Friday evening Tom rang. 'Can I come and stay?' he asked. 'I could get the train down tomorrow morning and be there by lunchtime.'

'OK,' I said, reluctant to relinquish my solitude and yet unable to say no.

I picked him up at the station and we drove out to the river Wye. We lay on the bank in the sunshine, chatting and catching up with each other's lives, before slipping into the cool, rippling water. A graceful arched stone bridge spanned the river and three young boys were happily diving off it. 'I still love you, Catherine,' Tom said, as we got ready to leave. 'Won't you please come home?' If only I could, I thought. If only I knew what that meant. I knew what Tom meant. He meant home to England, to him, to marriage. But deep down I knew that was not the kind of home I was longing for.

We had dinner outside in the garden. It was a perfect

summer night. The moon rose, golden and gleaming behind the trees, the scent of roses lingered in the warm evening air, candles flickered on the table and moths fluttered clumsily around our heads. Finishing a glass of wine, Tom reached across the table and took my hand. 'I just don't understand,' he said. 'What could you possibly find that is better than this?'

I sat looking at the dark silhouette of the barn and cottage, aware of the centuries of simple, domestic life that had been lived there. I looked at Tom across the table, his face so kind and loving, waiting expectantly for an answer. My mind raced: What is wrong with me? Why don't I get married and accept this is how life is? Why can't I just be normal? When my answer came, it burst out, surprising me as much as Tom.

'Everything,' I cried passionately. 'I want everything. I don't even know what that is, but I want it. I want to know who I am. I want to be able to stand in the centre of myself and say, "This is me." I can't commit myself to you or anyone until I can do that. When I finally discover who I really am, I might change beyond all recognition. You might not even like me or want to be with me! All I know,' I said, taking a deep breath, 'is that something deep within is calling and if I stop now I would betray myself, and I can't live with that.'

'You're impossible,' Tom said, sighing. He stood up, walked over, pulled me out of my chair and wrapped his arms around me. 'So you won't marry me. Can I hold you tonight anyway?'

When I dropped him off at the station the next day, saying goodbye was harder than ever. I drove home, parked the car and ran up the ridge.

'What am I doing?' I shouted out to the sky. 'For God's sake, tell me what on earth I am supposed to do? Should I get married?'

Quietly, inside, running deep as the deepest spring, calm and imperturbable, was the voice of my soul. 'No,' it said. 'Don't get married. Not now.'

'Really not?'

'Really not.'

I lay on the earth, my fingers digging down through the roots of the grass. I took a deep breath and let the truth sink in. No matter how hard it was to accept, in my bones, in my belly, I knew my soul was right.

That evening I was lying quietly in the bath, minding my own business, when the thing that I didn't even know could happen happened. Without thinking a thought, without making any effort or doing anything about it, the world dissolved. My body, the bath, the walls, the floor, house, trees, earth, stars, all dissolved into a sea of sparkling darkness, into an ocean of energy. Beyond space and time, past and future, here and there, this and that, I had dissolved into a state of pure being. Boundless and ineffable – it was the realm of the Absolute, the realm of infinite potential, of Spirit before it becomes manifest in the relative physical world as matter and form.

All that was left of me was awareness: consciousness stripped of all thoughts, all ideas, all illusions, all concepts of 'me' or 'I'. The whole paraphernalia gone in a second, leaving only the knowing. And in a flash I knew this was it. Knew that this realm of pure formless being was God. At least it was what people call God, for the sake of calling it something.

This is what people have been experiencing for thousands of years! I thought. Except I didn't think it, for it was not 'my' thought. It was simply the truth, which I had melted into. In the same way I understood that this realm I had entered was the source of all life and that the whole of existence, from insect to man to supernova, arises out of this realm of pure being and returns to it.

Floating in this boundless ocean of energy was utterly blissful: peace, joy, delight and ecstasy all rolled into one. All sense of 'me' disappeared, leaving only the feeling of reuniting and being at one with the Whole. Miraculously I had come back to my roots. I had come home to myself in the deepest possible way. Home to my true self. Not as an individual with a personality and particular set of characteristics, but to the realization that I was simply an expression of this greater Whole. As we all are. Momentary waves arising and falling on the ocean of Being.

As I revelled in the experience, I felt in the most profound way that this boundless energy we refer to as God is Love. Absolute, unconditional, limitless Love. Immeasurably beyond the scope of my everyday human experience and imagining. And yet not, for I had felt this Love so many times. In moments of tenderness and compassion, when my heart had cracked open at the beauty of the world, or with a lover, or my family and friends. I had felt this same Love without knowing it for what it really was.

But whereas it flickered on and off in my heart, I knew that the force of Love I now felt was eternal, ever present, everywhere. It was this Love that I had experienced so briefly standing in the kitchen when I was eight years old, caught in the middle of my parents' row. It was this Love

I had felt in the mountains, in my NLP training, in yoga. It was what I had longed for, searched for and strived to live by, throughout my whole life, without fully understanding why. Now I knew. This Divine Love was the 'everything' I had instinctively been so determined to find.

I felt inspired – filled with devotion, reverence, gratitude, humility, compassion and a deep sense of morality. Not man's morality with a capital 'M' and all its notions of sin and wickedness. Instead this was the feeling of connecting with an innate force of simple goodness and kindness and justice, and it struck me that this was the central experience and inspiration for all our religions.

I understood that our religious traditions – be they Christian, Hindu, or Muslim – were simply different ways of trying to translate the direct experience of God into something that we could all understand. Firstly, by teaching us how to connect with the presence of God through the many different forms of prayer, ritual, meditation and study. And secondly as a way of attempting to recreate, through moral codes and ways of living, this divine state of Love in our daily human lives.

Whether they have succeeded was another matter. For I could see the gap between the experience itself and the translation into the human realm, with all its distorted, bigoted ideas, and rules and regulations. I felt a sudden pang of compassion for mankind. For how hard we try and how much we still have to learn. I wanted to gather humanity up into my arms, the way a mother would soothe and comfort a troubled child and say, 'It will be OK. It is already OK. Really. Everything is going to be just fine.' For I realized that even though the pain and suffering and cruelty of our world is so great, it is not necessarily wrong, because it has the capacity to teach us so much. It is also temporal. Not an illusion exactly and yet, like a dream, it will pass and in the end all things will be restored to the Absolute.

Slowly the world began to re-materialize around me. I got out of the bath that had so recently dissolved, dried and dressed my body that had not existed and wandered out into the garden, gazing up into the dark sky full of stars, so similar and yet so different from the sparkling darkness I had just experienced. Everything was the same, but I was completely different. I felt as if I was suspended between two worlds. My consciousness was still imbued with the awareness of pure formless being and yet it was also here in this world of solid, material form. I gazed around me with new eyes, seeing things for the first time as they really are: the energy of God made manifest.

I woke up the next morning straight back into that place of clarity and joy. Everything is God. I looked at my hands, pale against the dark-green sheets, at the walls of the barn, at a wasp struggling against the window-pane, at the rays of light filtering through the trees, and at the walnut tree that had been my companion for these last few days. Everything is God. I wandered into the garden, the chill of dew against my feet, the warmth of the early-morning sun on my skin, and picked the last few berries from a raspberry bush, tasting the sweet scarlet crush of juice in my mouth. Everything is God. I listened to the birds singing, to the sounds coming from the nearby farm-yard and the soft voices of my neighbours in their garden. Everything is God.

Or perhaps I should say that God is everything. For

God is the whole – both visible and invisible, form and formlessness, immanent and transcendent. It is all just a great dance, I thought, as I spun around looking at the garden. A cosmic dance of Spirit and form, ebbing and flowing, becoming and dissolving, all arising from and returning to the state of pure being. Or a glorious experiment. Each created thing arising out of the ocean of infinite possibilities we call God, so that God can experience itself in a multitude of different forms. I bent down to watch a snail, oozing its way along the sturdy green stem of a spinach leaf. 'Are you?' I asked it. 'Are you part of a great experiment?' I looked at the exquisite patterns and colours of its shell and the answer was self-evident. Surely, I thought, in the end it is very simple. It is all the movement of Love. God is Love, manifesting itself in physical form, including human beings, so that we in return can celebrate and love Love.

I stood up and gazed out into the valley, feeling awed by the beauty, the magnificence, the extraordinary genius hidden in even the most ordinary of things. Even in me. I remembered all the times, the endless years, that I had spent worrying about whether I was good enough, and I burst out laughing because I saw finally, fatally, the ridiculousness of it. As if there can be anything or anyone that isn't intrinsically good enough.

With a shock I realized the huge ramifications caused by not knowing who and what we truly are. Not just the personal misery and self-hatred, but the wars, the exploitation and persecution, the destruction of entire cultures because they are different, the annihilation of other species because they seem less than. So much hatred. So much violence. None of this need happen, I thought; none of it could happen if we recognized and honoured the presence of Spirit in ourselves and in all other living things. The pain and destruction seemed so crazy and unnecessary that I struggled for a moment, trying to find my balance on the fulcrum between hope and despair.

Oh well, I sighed deeply, I guess we are all learning. We are like children, learning to recognize the truth. Learning to love. At least I hope so, for love is the only answer, the only way out of the cycle of hatred and violence. And maybe this is all part of the experiment. The 'Will they wake up before they completely destroy themselves?' part. And if we don't, perhaps it doesn't even matter, because ultimately there is nothing to lose – all things will return to the realm of pure being anyway. Yet here on earth, I thought, starting to appreciate the paradox in which we live, it does matter. How we live and what we do are of the greatest possible importance.

I picked a last raspberry, went into the cottage and put the kettle on to boil. I tore up some leaves of lemon balm, picked from a nearby stream and put them into a mug. I sliced bread into thick slices and put them in the toaster. The kettle boiled and I poured water into the mug. The fresh scent of lemon curled up on the steam. The toast popped and I slathered it with peanut butter, sat down at the table and chewed with relish, as I began to integrate what was happening to me.

Specific events from my life began to present themselves for re-evaluation. I remembered the guided meditation with Gary and dissolving into the river of universal knowledge. Next I remembered going to see Robert's Sufi friends, Ronnie and Rachel, at their house in London. I remembered asking what they meant by the 'veil' and the man who answered: 'One day you might be able to see through the veil of the material world altogether and experience God as transcendent – invisible, intangible, infinite.' Now I understood exactly what he meant by 'the veil' and 'God as transcendent'. Oh, I have been so blind, I thought. All this time I, the atheist, have been looking for God – the very thing I had most contempt for!

So why didn't I know this sooner? Why couldn't I see the truth even when it was pointed out to me? First of all, I realized it was because of a lack of education and understanding. As a child growing up during the Seventies and early Eighties on the Isle of Wight, no one in my social circle talked about spiritual life or waking up or the possibility of living with love and reverence. It was as if spirituality didn't exist and as a result I had no context in which to place my longing and no vocabulary with which to articulate my own fledgling sense of the sacred.

So even though I was desperately searching for truth and love and wholeness, it never occurred to me that meant I was on a spiritual path, because I didn't know that spirituality existed as something separate from religion. And I obviously wasn't religious because being religious meant you had to believe in God, which was my second problem. In my mind God had been reduced to such an absurdity – the bearded old man in the sky, deciding our fate and doling out punishment – that I couldn't possibly believe in it.

I pushed aside my breakfast things and grabbed a piece of paper. I made a list of all the associations I had with the word God. 'An old man' came at the top, but then came jealous, judgemental, repressive, punishing, sectarian; followed by all the terrible things that had been done and continue to be done in God's name. I compared that with what I now knew God to be – not an old man at all, but the pure, formless being that is the infinite source of life and unconditional love. How utterly tragic, I thought: that first list is all man's doing. None of it has anything to do with God.

So that was reason number two – my concept of God. Yet the truth, the real God, had been there all along. I remembered all the times I'd been in nature – in the mountains in Oregon, in the Grand Canyon, even here standing up on the ridge – and seen the light and beauty that is present in all things and felt the interconnectedness of life. But because my definition of God was so narrow and rigid, I couldn't put two and two together and see that light and beauty for what it really was!

I got up and put the kettle back on. As I walked across the kitchen I caught sight of my reflection in a little mirror that hung on a beam in the kitchen. I was surprised to see that I still looked the same, even though on the inside I was going through such a huge transformation. When the kettle boiled I made more tea and went outside. I sat on a weathered wooden bench and watched the birds at the bird-table. Finches, blue tits and a couple of adorable robins, all in a flurry of feathers and fluttering as they alighted, pecked at the seed and flew away again. Everything is God.

It is so obvious, it suddenly dawned on me: I have been on my path all along. For life itself is the path. Our spiritual nature is not separate from who we are, it *is* who we are and therefore life is by definition a spiritual journey, whether we know it or not. I got up and turned on the hose and began watering the flowerbeds – roses, lavender, daisies, rosemary, tarragon and parsley. Clouds drifted across a blue, blue sky. Birdsong filled the air. Everything is God.

So it is all a question of identity, I thought, of realizing who we really are. Because by waking up from our ego or false sense of self and learning to embody our soul or true nature, that place in us of deepest love and wisdom and truth, we are learning to embody God, the source of that deepest love and wisdom and truth. And in that way the light and love of God is manifest in the world, each of us expressing it in our own unique way.

I finished watering, sat down under the walnut tree with my diary, and began writing, attempting to do the impossible and capture the ineffable experience of God in words. There was a sudden commotion in the back of my mind. Like the Terminator, dragging itself from the wreckage of a massive explosion that is supposed to have finally, once and for all, completely destroyed it, my inner tyrant staggered to its feet.

'You cannot be serious about this whole God thing,' the tyrant said, scathing, sceptical and disgusted.

My ego poked its head out nervously from around the back of the tyrant. 'This is not going to go down well,' it added, in what sounded like a coaxing tone. 'Dad and Geoff are not going to like this.'

'No one is going to like it,' the tyrant butted in, 'if you start babbling about God. We're going to be ridiculed! Outcast! We're going to lose love!'

I felt a sudden chill of terror. For that, of course, was my greatest fear – the fear of not being loved. It was the very thing my ego had tried to protect me from all along by persuading me to conform and fit in, so that when

my father encouraged me to be logical, rational and intellectual, I had forced my innate spirituality into hiding. So
that is the third reason, I thought: no wonder I have been
trying so desperately to keep this part of me hidden. And
at the same time, I have been just as desperately looking
for it.

I lay on the ground and looked up through the pattern
of leaves, switching my focus from leaf to sky and back
again, as I thought about my father. If I have been moulded
by him, who was he moulded by? I wondered. Suddenly
I could see us both as the product of the greater society
in which we lived. From Descartes on, I thought, we have
been taught that life and the universe is merely physical,
material and mechanical. All trace of the metaphysical or
spiritual has been severed from our lives in a triumph of
logical thinking. At what a great cost! To me. To my dad.
To everyone.

A wave of grief swept through my body, as I felt how
much this denial and hiding had hurt me. The fear and
the loneliness it had created. The bewildering emptiness
of life when it is robbed of its deeper meaning. Not to
mention the self-hatred and shame I had lived with. 'For
what?' I cried out bitterly. 'For my spirit, my true self.
The most beautiful and precious thing there is in anyone.
Now that's what I call stupid!'

The grief subsided and I sat up, resting my back against
the trunk of the walnut tree. In spite of my ego's fear I
knew there was no going back. I knew I had been given
a priceless gift and I felt sure it had not been given to me
just for my own private pleasure, but entrusted to me to
use wisely and share with other people.

'Is that right?' I asked my soul, secretly hoping for a

reprieve. 'Am I meant to share this experience in some way?'

'Yes,' said my soul. 'Speak of God as Love. That's all you need to do. Speak of God as Love.'

I thought of all the great religious and spiritual teachers, such as Christ, Buddha, Muhammad, Rumi, and of the thousands of priests, monks and devotees who had followed in their footsteps. I thought of all the great mystics and artists, the painters, composers and poets, who had attempted to communicate the direct experience of God through their art. And I thought: Who the hell am I? Who am I, compared to all these enlightened and gifted beings, that I could possibly have anything to contribute to what has already been said?

'You know exactly who you are,' replied my soul, in a gentle reprimand. 'You are an expression of God. Through you God manifests in a unique way. Only you can give voice to that experience, and this is your true purpose. This is what really matters, that each person and each creature embody and express their natural divinity and so add their voice to the universal love song that is God.'

'OK,' I said, 'I'll try.'

2